Just Tell Me I'm Pretty

Nothing is too private, too embarrassing or too heart-wrenching for Heather LeRoss to share. Honesty with lots of humor make Just Tell Me I'm Pretty a book to read again and again."

—Jen Mann, New York Times Best Selling Author of *Working with People I Want to Punch in the Throat*

Heather LeRoss writes for every woman and does so while bringing forth every emotion.

—Bunmi Laditan, author of *Confessions of a Domestic Failure*

LeRoss brings you into the heart of her world with fearless, relatable honesty, affirming that despite all your bumblings and failures, the one thing you are not, is alone."

—Kristen Mae, bestselling author of *Red Water*

Just Tell Me I'm Pretty

Published by Kat Biggie Press.
Columbia, SC 29229
http://katbiggiepress.com

Cover design by Michelle Fairbanks, Fresh Design
Cover Art by Adrienne Hedger
Book design by Alexa Bigwarfe, Write | Publish | Sell
www.writepublishsell.co
Editing by Stacey Aaronson

ISBN-13: 978-0-9994377-3-5
Library of Congress Control Number: 2017957117
First Edition: November 2017

10 9 8 7 6 5 4 3 2 1

Just Tell Me I'm Pretty

Musings on a Messy Life

Heather LeRoss

Kat Biggie Press
Columbia, SC USA

This word baby is dedicated to my real babies, Aidan and Gavin. You'll always be my baby boys.

Thank you for opening my heart to a world of love like I've never known.

Introduction

I'm a mom. If you're reading this book, I imagine you're a mom too. Or you want to be. Or you know a mom, had a mom . . . you get it.

Besides being a mom (which is enough), I'm also a healer, a superhero, a magician, a yeller, a crier, and a believer. I'm a mom to two boys—one with Attention Deficit Hyperactivity Disorder (ADHD), and one who often lives in the shadow of ADHD.

This book is written for any woman who has cared for a child, whether biological, adopted, step, or friend. It is for each of you who have loved so wholeheartedly that sometimes it feels like you can't hold any more love in your heart. It is for those of you who have given tirelessly to a child—watching them grow, struggle, and overcome—and held your breath with each step. It's for the woman who has felt completely alone in her mothering journey. For the woman who has hidden in her closet and cried, because sometimes, that is all she could do. To the woman who nursed a sick child 'round the clock, who gave every ounce of energy and love she had and never expected a thank you in return.

This is a thank you to you, for your love, your guidance, and your selflessness. This is also future payback for my two sons, who still ask me to wipe their butts, and who threaten to drive me insane with fart wars, pee stains, and their stink.

This book is also for the mothers of special-needs children, who attend endless parent-teacher meetings about their atypical child. To the moms who sit through those meetings, heart racing and holding back tears, because it's just too much to hear how her child is "lacking/falling behind/disruptive/lazy." To those moms who tenaciously fight to get their child the help they need, so that their awesomeness can shine through.

My hope is that someday, this won't be a fight. That we will unite in our desire to support one another and help our children thrive, whether it's co-sleeping or not, breast or bottle, meds or no meds. To ensure our children grow, learn, and live in ways that suit *them* best. To be a safe place for each other in our journey, without the need to tear anyone down for doing things differently. To applaud ourselves. To embrace our children's quirks and differences, and to make them feel "normal."

I hope this book helps. I hope you know how awesome you are for waking every day and continuing to do your best. I hope you understand how remarkable you are, how amazing your child is, and that neither of you is "lacking." They are perfect and so are you.

We're all warriors battling for our children to have the best life possible. Soldier on, Momma. I am with you.

Some people write bestsellers. Some people save lives. I just spent 23 minutes looking for the glasses on my head.

Chapter 1

Dear Neighbor: I'm Sorry

It all started when I was on Pinterest looking for a hostess gift to take to an upcoming holiday party. The neighborhood is new; we're all recently transplanted residents getting to know one another, and I was hoping to find something simple but ahhhmazing to make and take. Because yes, I admit that I care about what my neighbors think and am hoping to make a good impression. Especially after some of the things that have happened since my gang of boys and I moved in.

As I was looking at fun crafts to make with extra wine glasses (because for some reason, I have a shit ton of extra wine glasses), I realized what I should really do is write an apology letter to some of the neighbors for the things they might have noticed around our crib. It should probably be sent along with wine, since I'm sure my gaggle has driven more than a few people to drink.

I decided I would put a humorous spin on the goings-on in my hood, so I wrote this letter:

Dear New Neighbor—Please Let Me Explain,

I wanted to apologize for not stopping by to say a proper hello and welcome. I feel terrible for being so rude. I saw you wave this morning, and I wanted you to know that I was trying to wave back. Turns out I hadn't put the lid on my coffee mug correctly, and as I raised my hand (and coffee mug) to say hi, it spilled all over my lap. Ouch! THAT was why you heard me drive by and exclaim, "Oh for fuck's sake, you're an idiot!" That was NOT directed at you but I can understand how, with my window rolled down, making eye contact with you and then belting that out, you might think it was directed at you. I was late to an appointment because the dog had decided it was the perfect moment to roll around in his own shit, which I had to clean up before leaving. I was frazzled, which explains why the lid was not tightly on my mug.

After this exchange, and the ones previously (blush), I thought a note of explanation was warranted so you don't end up quickly moving to the other side of the street when walking by, or telling your kids they can't come play at the weird neighbor's house.

Last weekend, when I was walking my dog, I did wave (yay, me!) and noticed an odd look on your face when you waved back. I assumed you were just a little snooty and rude. It wasn't until I got home that I realized I was wearing my pink rhinestone-studded tiara. That might have looked a little crazy. See, my son bought me the tiara for Christmas one year and told me it made him sad that I never wore it. In truth, I hadn't been able to find it and was unpacking a box from our move (over a year ago) and found it! So I put it on to make him happy, then forgot I had it on and took the dog for a walk. I am NOT a woman who routinely wears a tiara to walk the dog, but I can understand how you might not believe that. Well, I guess I AM that woman but, well, you get it. I'll need to let the other neighbors know too. Who would have thought it would be THAT night that I meet five of our new neighbors!

I also wanted to explain the conversation you heard in the backyard the other day. As you've seen, I have three boys between the ages of seven and twelve. It gets a little wild here! Despite what you heard me yell, I wasn't literally going to duct tape my son's butt-hole shut if he didn't stop farting on his brother's head. I mean, I would love to (since the farts can seem endless), but I would never REALLY do that.

And when you heard me yell, "If you ask me to come and wipe your butt one more time, I'm going to make you start wiping mine!" . . . well, that was just the frustration talking. I am completely capable of wiping my own butt, and of course would never make my son do that. I just get tired of telling my twelve-year-old to wipe his own butt. You get it, right?

I also feel the need to explain what my eldest told you the other day when you came to borrow our ladder. Evidently, he told you he couldn't ask me because I was having Mommy's Naked Time. See, the only way to ensure my boys don't barge into my room looking for me is to tell them I'm naked. Then they knock. So sometimes on a Sunday afternoon, I escape into my room to play a little Candy Crush—I tell them I'm dressing and naked. I only take a half hour or so, but I guess they have now dubbed it Mommy's Naked Time. Ha, ha, boys. You can come borrow the ladder tonight if you still need it.

Finally, I am so sorry for this afternoon, when my youngest came to your house asking if you knew where I was. I know you were a bit panicked, but everything was okay, really. He and his brother had been fighting all afternoon. When I went into the bathroom to yell at them to stop, they were having a "sword fight"—with their pee. I kind of lost it. I wasn't sure how I was going to get the pee off the ceiling, and the dog was standing there licking the floor. I just needed to be alone. I told them all to go to their rooms and I hid in my closet. Sometimes I hide in there, where everything smells clean and it's dark and no one can find me. I guess my youngest decided to come looking for me and freaked when he couldn't find me. I'm sorry he frightened you so much that you felt compelled to call the police. I don't know where he came up with the idea that I had been kidnapped.

I'm really a very nice woman and usually a very good neighbor. I would love to have you over for dinner. I think the kids will get along better. I've talked to my boys about never using the dried dog poo in the back-yard as bullets in their Nerf guns, so that shouldn't be an issue if the kids play Nerf wars again. I am so sorry your kids had to go through that.

Let me know if you're free soon and we'll plan something. I have lots of wine to choose from. Or beer. We also have rum, vodka, te-quila, and well, we can find something you might like.

Sincerely,
Your New Neighbors

Hell hath no fury like a little brother who can't reciprocate a fart on his brother's head.

Chapter 2
I'm Going to Remember (and Record) EVERY Moment!

I have been writing since I was eight, when I decided to pen my first book (yes, you heard correctly). I wrote a story about my grandfather's horse, Rhoney, and me. It was amazingly brilliant (if I do say so myself) and surely would have won me some awards had I not lost it. So, sadly there is no proof of my young genius, but trust me, it was great!

I've loved writing stories and poems for as long as I can remember. I majored in English Literature in college, amazed that they would give me college credit for reading good books and writing. Score! So, when I found out I was pregnant with my first child, I was going to be "that mom" who chronicles the whole journey. I was going to relish each day, not only of pregnancy, but also the whole journey of motherhood. I would keep track of everything, all the firsts, the funnies, the heart tugs, and the lasts. It would be recorded so that later I could create a beautifully bound book for my daughter, which would then be handed down through the generations.

The following is my journey, which I hope you enjoy.

July 15, 2002

Oh, holy shit! Just took a pregnancy test and it was positive! Guess this explains the bad acne and exhaustion lately. A baby! I think I'm still in shock. Dan is beside himself with excitement—he's called everyone we know. I'm expecting a sign in our yard announcing it soon. Just kidding. Okay, have to go, we're going out to celebrate. A baby! Aaaack!

July 29, 2002

I'm going to try and write more often now. But I've felt wretched. I don't have morning sickness, I have ALL-DAY sickness. I feel good for about an hour in the afternoon and that's it. Dan has been traveling the past two weeks, which is good, because I'm not great company. I think it's a girl. Actually, I'm sure of it because (this is dumb, I know) I HAVE to have a girl. I'm a girly girl. I like pink and shiny and princesses and would be a horrible boy mom. Mom is sure I'm having a girl too. And don't girls make you have extra estrogen? That's probably why I have all the acne. I want to write more but feel like poo right now . . .

Oct. 31, 2002

Okay, not so great at writing. But the good news is, the morning (all-day) sickness has finally stopped! I'm craving fruit, grilled cheese sandwiches, and Blizzards from DQ. Not too bad healthwise, except I can never choose between the Oreo Blizzard or the strawberry one. Dan brings home both, and I choose which I'll have right then and save the other for the next day. Well, that's my plan anyway. So far, none have made it into the freezer until the next day. They both end up in my belly! One for me, one for the baby! Ha!

I don't want to gain a ton of weight, but I'm hungry all the time. Work sucks, and Dan has been traveling nonstop, but it's okay because I'm pregnant! All looks good and I'm due April 6. I'm hoping she'll be early or late since Dan's birthday is the 7th and that would be a bit much. Especially since Mom's birthday is the 19th. April is going to be a busy month.

Oh, I'm positive it's a girl. We call her Spud (but I call her Ashley in my head—weeeee!). I'm seeing all these adorable baby Halloween costumes. I think for her first Halloween, Ashley will be a lady-bug—too cute!

Nov. 12, 2002

I've gained 15 lbs. I think that's normal though, right? I found the perfect room décor for Ashley. It's pink and green and yellow, lacy, girly, and all things PERFECT! I'm holding off buying for now, because that would be a little crazy, given I am not sure (okay, I SO am) that it's a girl.

Acne sucks and so does the gas.

Nov. 18, 2002

Ugh, I gained five more pounds. I find out in three days what we're having! I am addicted to Babycenter and the pregnancy board. Bunch of women all over the world, all due in April 2003. My saving grace right now. And, I think finding this board and all these ladies is an omen, because almost all of them are having girls! I'm fat but again, that's okay because I'm PREGNANT!!! Right? Right.

Okay, I swear I will write more soon . . .

Nov. 22, 2002

It's a boy.

Dec. 23, 2002

Okay, I've adjusted to the whole boy thing. I feel like a wretched mother now, though. Who cries in front of the nurse when they find out they're having a healthy baby boy? But I don't know much about boys. I watched my nephews, but I'm pretty sure James is gay (he played with Polly Pockets, watched Disney princesses, wore his hair long, and called his underwear his "panties"), and Kyle was still a baby. What about when he grows up?? Dan is excited of course—now he'll have a gaming buddy. They changed my due date when I went in last time, so now it's April 11. They explained why but I don't remember. I was so pissed that it meant I would have to work for one more week. Hate my job. Hate my boss. Love my big ole belly, though.

There are cute boy things out there . . . somewhere. Right?

p.s. I've gained a total of 25 lbs. Shhhh

Jan. 8, 2003

I cannot believe he will be here in about three months! Room is not ready yet, and Dan is hardly ever home because of work. I did find cute room décor, with blue and yellow and stars and moons. Oh, and I finally took back the pink onesies, hair bows, and little ballet shoes. I didn't tell anyone I had bought them. It was hard taking them back, but I consoled myself with a one-pound box of See's candy and a new robe. I also picked out some cute green and yellow boy clothes. Funny how the boys' clothing section (even for babies) is like one-third the size of the girls' section.

I'm not sure how this traveling job for Dan is going to work once Spud is here. Of course, I'm hoping he gets a better job and then maybe I can stay home with Spud! I think I'd make a fantastic housewife. :-) Job still sucks. Only three more months!

Feb. 16, 2003

Long time no write. Been busy. Dan has been traveling a lot (what else is new), and I've been getting stuff for Spud. I think we've decided on a name—Aidan. I love it! And the BEST part is we only know one other person with an Aidan. I don't think it's a popular name, which is good. We wanted something a little different. I feel him kick and move all the time now. He gets the hiccups a lot, which I love. But I think his foot is lodged under my boob, which is hurting like a motherfucker!

And I can't poop. If I could, I'd lose some of this weight, I'm sure. I've gained 30 lbs.

March 1, 2003

Had my baby shower and it was awesome! Friends really outdid themselves and I felt the love. I have so much cute stuff for Aidan. I'm getting a bit stressed because the room isn't done, but Dan swears next weekend when he's home, he'll get it painted and the crib together. I moved all the boxes and crap out. We have so much crap. Aidan's foot is still stuck under my boob. I'm ready to have him out.

I need to poop.

March 25, 2003

I pooped!!!

March 27, 2003

Oh My God, the waiting is unbearable! I'm huge, so huge, my boss said in a meeting the other day, "Wow, you're HUGE. I mean, I know you're pregnant, but you're huge!" I wanted to say, "Yeah, well I'll have this baby and not be HUGE, but you'll still be a bitch." I didn't. I smiled. I also smiled when she said my acne was so bad, it looked like I had chicken pox. This is a woman who comes to work with her clothes on inside out and announces she's decided to stop brushing her hair. Get me out of there.

I've gained 35 lbs. I'm done with the scale.

March 29, 2003

So, boss tells me the other day that she cannot guarantee I'll have a job when I come back from maternity leave. She says she just doesn't know what to do with me. Ummm, pretty sure that's illegal. Have I mentioned how much I dislike her? I'm counting down the days. It's getting pretty uncomfortable now. Good news is the room is coming along. It's painted and looks cute. I'm doing the finishing touches in the next week and we will be set! Starting to get pretty nervous about the actual birth, but I took a hypno-birthing class so I should be set. It's all about focusing on something to get you through the pain. And breathing. I bought a cute Winnie the Pooh porcelain figure to take with me and focus on. Then, I figure, it will look cute in Aidan's room and will always hold special memories.

I'm not opposed to drugs, though . . .

April 6, 2003

This was supposed to be my due date. He's not here. I'm still at work. Room is done. His foot is still under my boob, and I think my skin might split open. I'm huge. I need to poop, which I hear might happen on the table. As gross as that is, I'm kinda looking forward to it.

April 11, 2003—11:59 p.m.

HE'S NOT HERE! I mean, I know the due date is a best estimate, but HE'S NOT HERE! I'm done. I need him out. I'm ready. I walked today, ate spicy food, ate pineapple. I'm so uncomfortable and ready to just have him out. I'm ready to meet him and hold him and be done with work. I bought those giant-sized muffins from Costco the other day. There were 16. There are only five left. Oh, and I am horribly addicted to *Dawson's Creek* and this designing show. I can't sleep, so I eat muffins, watch *Dawson's* reruns, and find ways to declutter and decorate my house. I figure I'll have some time once Aidan is here, and maybe I can get some of the shit done I've been meaning to do for ages.

I'm going to make a grilled cheese and tomato sandwich. I'm not telling anyone, but I eat about four of those a day now. Screw the weight . . . I can lose it after Aidan is here. Not like I was a skinny Minnie before I got prego.

April 12, 2003

He's. Not. Here.

April 13, 2003

Hey, guess what? No f*%king baby yet! I'm off work now, which I should be enjoying, but I am so damned uncomfortable, I mainly just walk the neighborhood, watch *Dawson's Creek*, and try to nap and poop. I'm so tired and frustrated. I'm having contractions all the time, but the fake ones. Fake contractions. Like women don't have it hard enough with this whole baby thing.

Desperate, Dan and I actually had sex today. Awkward. I won't even go into detail. But so awkward. I heard sex can stimulate things and push you into labor. It better work, because I'm not doing it again. Did I mention it was a bit awkward???

April 14, 2003—4 a.m.

OMG OMG! It's happening! I woke up at one something, with contractions that were uncomfy enough to wake me and make it so I couldn't go back to sleep. I've been in the bath for a bit and now downstairs with a muffin. *Dawson's Creek* is on (seriously, this show plays like 24 hours a day). Dan is still asleep. I figure, why wake him yet? They're not horrible. I'm timing them and they're still 10 minutes apart. But getting closer and stronger. Nothing too bad, though.

7 a.m. Definitely closer—about five minutes now and stronger. Dan is still sleeping, but I'm going to wake him soon. I love Katie Holmes.

8 a.m. Okay . . . woke Dan, he's taking a bath.

He's all calm but I'm starting to get nervous. I'm not sure I'm ready for the pain. And then the whole "being a mom" thing! Going to call doc soon and see what I do next . . .

8:24 a.m. Doc said come in for exam! I think this is happening! It hurts. The muffins are all gone.

The End.

That's as far as I got. Aidan is 14 now and this about sums up my journaling the days of motherhood.

p.s. Hypno-birthing was a joke, and the cute little Winnie the Pooh figurine ended up breaking when I threw it against the wall.

Everything is sticky. It smells funny in here. I'm tired.
—Autobiography of a mom

Chapter 3

Baby #2

(THIS time, I'm going to record and remember every moment.)

There are a lot of April birthdays in my family. My mom, my ex-husband, Aidan, and even though mine is in May, it's the 4th, so it's still really close to April. My only stipulation when my husband and I talked about trying for baby #2 (our girl) was that she not be born in April.

We had decided we wouldn't go all out "trying," but that I would go off the pill and we'd see what happened. If I wasn't pregnant within the year, my husband would have a vasectomy.

I was pregnant two weeks later.

With the same EXACT SAME due date I'd had for Aidan (who was three days late)—April 11th.

Well, shit.

I decided this time I would do a much better

job of journaling throughout my pregnancy. Here you go!

July 25, 2007

I'm pregnant again! I knew it when I saw the acne again and dozed off in a meeting. Isn't pregnancy grand? This time, I'm going to be much better about keeping record of my pregnancy. I really want to have something to give Ashley when she's older. Yes, I am positive this time it's a girl. So, get this, little girl, you have the exact same due date as your older brother! Isn't that crazy? It's crazy. Okay, I need to go help Aidan wipe his butt. More soon!

August 15, 2007

Ack! I let a little too much time slip by between entries. Life has been hectic, what with the morning (or all-day) sickness again and trying to stay on top of work, Aidan, and life. I still can't believe I have the same due date for both my kids.

This time around, work is MUCH better. I work from home now so that helps. I can sneak away for a nap when I need it, which lately, is every afternoon. I'm staying on top of work, so I don't feel bad. I finally had to admit, though, that I'm not having a girl. Don't ask me how I know, I just know I'm having boy #2. I guess reality hit, with the fact that hubby has two brothers, his dad is one of three boys, and your uncle has three boys. So yeah, you're a boy. BUT, this is pretty cool since we saved a lot of the baby stuff from Aidan. Except the furniture. I could kick myself for that, given that I JUST sold it a month before getting prego. Now we have to buy all new but that's okay. You'll have plenty of hand-me-downs!

Okay, gotta go get Aidan a snack. More soon!

Dec. 16, 2007

You're a boy. If I were a betting woman, I'd be rich.

I feel horrible for not writing more but . . . well, I have no good excuse, except working FT, having Aidan, managing life. My New Year's resolution is to be better, so watch out—2008 will have a whole journal full of thoughts, feelings, happenings, and such for you to read someday!

Feb. 24, 2008

Ummm, I'm not doing much better at writing. I'm so sorry, baby boy! Being pregnant takes a lot out of me, and I've been dealing with some butt issues lately. Namely, you've given me a horrid case of hemorrhoids! Sorry, I know that's gross. But this is a journal of memories for me too. I guess I shouldn't really want to remember the horror that sitting is for me right now. Okay, I'll write more later. I need to nap.

Gavin is nine now, and this is as far as I got in my journal. Maybe this book will suffice.

Found a happy face sticker stuck to my boob when I took off my bra. In case you wondered what sexy looks like.

Chapter 4

I Soiled Myself in IKEA

(a cool story about a little talked about joy of pregnancy)

I released the Kraken in IKEA.

In my defense, it happened during my last week of pregnancy with Gavin. If you've ever carried a human being inside of you, you know the level of mortification, grossness, and discomfort that comes along with it. You feel me, right?

I have a love/hate thing with IKEA. On one hand, I love the bargains and the cool things I don't need but OH MY GOD, I WANT! I also enjoy the cinnamon rolls and the meatballs. I like wandering the odd aisles, sitting in the room displays, imagining it's my house—my perfectly clean, organized house where the kids are hidden, everything is in its place, and it smells like cinnamon rolls all day.

On the other hand, I hate the crowds of slow,

meandering people with their 600 kids. They stop to look at everything, and sometimes they're so rude as to lie on the bed I was just about to plunk down on and rest my feet.

This particular trip was fraught with peril from the beginning. My (now-ex) husband (this story was not the reason for our marriage failure, but I would have understood if it had been) and I had decided to take Aidan to get final things for the baby's room and have lunch. The problem was, I was a week away from delivery and had been dealing with the worst constipation and hemorrhoids of my life. Like this shit was so bad (haha, I jest, there was NO shit), I'd recently gone to see a surgeon about possible 'roid removal. Oh, this was a fun visit!

(Begin wavy dream sequence music and visual here)

Visiting the butt doctor, I was the lucky pregnant woman who got to be there on "intern" day.

"Do you mind if the two interns sit in on the exam?" they asked, in all seriousness.

WTF? Was this a cruel joke they played on pregnant women? Or were they trying to make the fact that I was in a doctor's office, having my BUTT

LOOKED AT a little *more* mortifying?

I waited for the "Just kidding! Now isn't this visit better, since you only have one doctor looking at your backside?"

Those words never came. They just stared at me, waiting for my answer.

I should have said, "No way in hell!" but instead out came "The more the merrier!" That's when they sent my husband out of the room, because the doctor said, "No man needs to see his wife in this position."

I ended up not getting the surgery, but the memory will last forever.

(End wavy dream sequence music and visual)

I digress. The trip needed to happen, so I put on my big girl panties (seriously, they were BIG), put in a Preparation H plug, and slathered the whole area with witch hazel cream. I donned my prettiest and sexiest maternity sweats—the light gray ones—and off we went. I had my doughnut for sitting (bless the doughnut), so the ride was a joy.

As we were walking in, it happened. The gas. Anyone who has used suppositories knows that they often cause gas. Determined to forge ahead, I stayed away from people, letting out little puffs as I went. I tooted my way through the aisles, grabbing stuff left and right.

When nature called, I took Aidan to the restroom and was appalled. As I squatted in the stall to give my back a rest, I exploded from my backside. It was so loud, my son jumped and started giggling, and the woman in the stall next to us couldn't suppress a laugh. I give her credit for trying. I heard the sweetest voice say, "Mommy, that was the loudest pouf I've ever heard!" Followed by, "Shhhhh."

I waited to leave until I thought everyone who'd heard was gone. We finished our shopping, got a cinnamon roll, and left. Once home, I was happy to feel the "urge" to make magic happen, so I waddled to the bathroom. Then I saw it: the stain. There was a HUGE oily, dark mark from my bottom, all the way down the back of the pant legs. On both sides. WTF? I looked closer and realized that with each toot, I had been expelling bits of the oily Prep H.

Really.

I can't explain the mortification, disgust, and downright defeat I felt. There was no hiding the stain; I'm quite sure everyone in IKEA noticed. I don't know how in the hell I didn't feel anything, but honestly, I was so effing sick and tired of thinking about my ass, I think it was numb.

This was pregnancy's final way of ripping me of my dignity and any hope of feeling attractive. And the absolute worst part was not that I had hundreds of strangers witness my leaky bum, it was that the oil from the suppository stained the pants. They were the only pants that fit, and now they were trash. I spent the next week in my husband's old sweats with no drawstring, which was fine, since my stomach was so huge they stayed up on their own.

I share this with you all in the hopes of solidarity among women—so that if there's another lady out there going through her own pregnancy horror, she can read this and not feel so alone. And, as a gentle reminder to not toot in public after suppository insertion.

Woke my son up this morning with kisses and proclamations of my undying love.

He rolled over and said, "Your breath stinks."

Chapter 5

They Said WHAT???

I am surrounded by males. Two boys of my own and a stepson. I also have my husband and a male dog. I am encompassed by testosterone and farts on a daily basis (my husband insists I clarify it is the boys and dogs who are farting), which means not only is my world boy-gross, it's loud, wild, chaotic, jittery, and hilarious.

As a result, I have developed what we'll call TONB, which is a syndrome spreading like wildfire in the Mommy community, but is widely under-diagnosed.

"TONB" syndrome: Testosterone Overload, Need Bubbles.

And when I say I need bubbles, I'm talking about any form of bubbles. Like being able to take a hot bath without anyone coming in saying, "Oh my God, I saw your boobies," or treating myself to a nice glass of Prosecco without someone asking,

"Can you smell the fart I just let? I can, it's bad. Here, does this help?" fanning the smell my way with his hand (again, NOT my husband. He's got more class than the boys).

If there is any question that TONB is real, let me assure you that for me, it is as real as taxes. Let me detail just a few of the things that have led to my TONB.

Farts:

"Mommy, I farted and the fart bubble is stuck in my butt."

"Mommy, Aidan farted on my head and said farts leave tiny poops behind. Get it off!"

"Hey, let's see if we can fill this balloon with farts."

"Mommy!!! I farted but it came out as poop."

"Boys, you do not fart at the table." Which then led to them stand up quickly and walk behind their chairs, farting and claiming, "But it wasn't at the table!"

"Mommy, I farted and it hurt my butt. I need to stay home from school."

Burps:

"Haha! My burp came out my butt." (Could also

be included in above section)

When reminding my boys not to burp at the table: "But if it stays inside, it will get bigger and I'll explode!"

A note home from school for my eldest:

Hi Heather,

There was an incident in our spelling lesson today, where I asked who could recite the whole alphabet. Aidan raised his hand and proceeded to belch out his ABCs. I was able to get him to stop by F, but the class was out of control laughing by then, and the rest of the lesson time was spent calming them down. When I tried to talk to Aidan about it, he said the burp was stuck in his brain, and that burping it out was the only way to get the letters out of his mouth.

Please remind Aidan, burping in class is not acceptable.

Have a great day!
Mrs. L

"Burps are Mother Nature's way of letting us

make a breeze." (Now this I thought was quite clever, but I still had to remind him that it was not okay to do in my friend Amber's face—even if she did say she needed more fresh air.)

The Penis:

"Mommy, look! My penis is hard and it's SO big!"

"Please don't put your dinosaurs in your penis hole!"

"No, YOU need fresh air. Your penis does not. We're at the park, pull your pants up!"

"Mommy, I have a boner! Make it stop!"

"Take the toilet paper off. Your penis is not a mummy!"

"No, your penis does NOT need a drink. Don't even think about putting it in your milk."

Boogers:

"Because wiping your boogers on your wall is gross, that's why."

"I understand it's show-and-tell today and the letter is B. That does not mean you show and tell about your boogers."

"Please stop picking your nose. No, your boogers are not lonely and need attention."

I could go on, but I'm sure you get the picture at this point. I'm surrounded by all things gross. And I simply long for a warm bath in a candlelit bathroom, with a glass of bubbly and a good book. And no, boys, I am not in the bathroom making my own bubbles. And no, you cannot come in and play in the bathwater with your toys. No, I don't want to see your penis do tricks, and no, I'm not impressed that you could burp Little Einstein's cartoon theme song. (Okay, well, that one might be a little cool.)

My son woke me from a nap this weekend to let me know I'd fallen asleep.

This is parenting.

Chapter 6

Kidsdom

My kids have a lot of wisdom. Just ask them, they'll tell you. They know it all, and they'll fight about who is right until Mommy jumps in and yells that if they don't stop, neither one will see the sky again, so they'll never solve the "It's blue. No, it's light-ish blue-gray" conundrum.

Here are just a few of the gems they impart. I call it *kidsdom*—wisdom, kid style.

12-yr.-old: "I'm so hot from walking home (lifts shirt to cool off). Ohhh, uh-oh, oh, one of my nipples is harder than the other!"

Me: (looks up to see son rubbing nipples)

12-yr.-old: "Oh wait, it's okay. They're both hard now."

Crisis averted.

* * * *

Practicing acts of kindness with my boys:

Me: "Let's try and do something kind for some-one today."

12-yr.-old: "I did. I pooped *and* flushed."

Me: . . .?

12-yr.-old: "You know, so you didn't have to."

* * * *

Me: "Why do you always have only two pairs of underwear in the laundry?"

12-yr.-old: "I'm thinking of you, Mom, trying to cut down on your work."

Me: "Ewww!"

12-yr.-old: "I turn them inside out!"

* * * *

7-yr.-old: "I saw something I want at the store."

Me: "What was it?"

7-yr.-old: "I'm not exactly sure what it is, but the box said Max iPad. Sounds cool."

Me: "We need to chat."

* * * *

7-yr.-old: "When I grow up, I'm going to marry Aly."

Me: "Oh, you like her, huh?"

7-yr.-old: "No, but she never eats all her lunch. Daddy says it's important to look for ways to save money."

Me: . . .

* * * *

At public pool:

12-yr.-old: "Look, Mom, I'm making my own bubbles!!"

* * * *

11-yr.-old: "I like how you smell."

Me: "Awww, how sweet."

11-yr.-old: "Ohhh, that fart I just let smells good too."

* * * *

Boy conversation in RV park PUBLIC shower:

11-yr.-old: "I need to pee."

12-yr.-old: "I just did."

11-yr.-old: "Look, I'm peeing on the wall!"

12-yr.-old: "Listen." (farts). "Ohhh, a wet one!"

* * * *

Recently, I was exclaiming how happy I was that my pants fit again.

12-yr.-old: "Yeah, but they make your butt look big."

Me: . . .

12-yr.-old: "I mean your hips. They make your hips look big."

Ummm, much better?

* * * *

My son spent the morning assuring me it was pajama day at day camp. It did not say this on the weekly itinerary, so I had doubts.

Me: "Are you SURE they said it's pajama day?"

7-yr.-old: (Rolling his eyes) "Mommy, I have short-term memory loss! Really. I think that's what they said, but how would I know?"

* * * *

Random bits of kidsdom:

11-yr.-old: "It's going to be a really good day. I know because my butthole hurts."

4-yr.-old: "I won't eat any broken chips, cracked fruit bars, or the skin on pickles."

4-yr.-old: "Ewww, the strawberries have pimples. Get them off!"

3-yr.-old: "No, Mommy, don't take him! He's my friiieeennnndd!" (huge, wet tears because I took the booger off his finger)

* * * *

Career day at school:

Me: "Why are you wearing your Iron Man costume for career day?"

6-yr.-old: "Because I want to be an actress." (rolls eyes "duh" style)

* * * *

11-yr.-old (to girl over for dinner he has a crush on): "Hahahaha! You have red stuff on your face and something stuck in your teeth. Wow, you sure eat a lot. *Beeellllccchhh*. 'Scuse me."

I know I have some time before the ecstasy comes that is age 18, but given my boys' track record, I'm not sure I'll ever experience them leaving home.

My son told me his goal in life
is to own a monkey and a turtle so
they can be "bro's."
Pretty sure I'll never experience
the "empty nest" syndrome.

Chapter 7

My Kids Are Weird

Tic-Tacs, makeup, baby dolls, tea sets, long hair, monkeys, and turtles—these are just a few of the things my boys have been into. Yes, my boys have been into makeup, tea sets, and baby dolls. And my eldest really did have an odd obsession with Tic-Tacs of all colors and flavors. Seriously, he once saved his allowance and spent $30 on a jumbo-sized box of Tic-Tacs that housed mini boxes of Tic-Tacs inside. From Slovenia. No kidding, he bid on it on eBay, won, and was beside himself with excitement.

My stepson has long hair, like really long, as does my ex-husband. My youngest son has decided long hair is cool and has refused haircuts. Since the boys haven't hit puberty yet, one of them is always mistaken for a girl. Always. The other one has really crazy "bad" long hair, and so I think he escapes being thought of as a girl, because most people know that no self-respecting girl would keep her long locks in such horrid form. I try to brush out the tangles and tame down the wild, weird curls, but it's an act of futility.

One of the boys recently spent his birthday money to buy two baby dolls, complete with blue and pink onesies, pacifiers, and moveable arms. The other boy has had a makeup obsession and would love nothing more than to spend all of his free time going through my makeup drawer, over and over, asking what each item is and how it's used. He says he loves the colors. He spent his allowance on an eyeshadow palette.

One of my boys is currently working on a paper in school to try and convince me to get him a turtle. He doesn't help much with our family dog, and the hamster he got a few years ago ended up not being quite as "fun" as he'd thought it would be. After he'd had it about a year, he asked his dad if they could take it back to the store. He wanted a lizard instead, because those would be super fun and of course he would totally take care of it, feed it, love it, and pet it. Thankfully, his dad said no and made him keep the hamster and take care of it, until it lost its battle with being "not fun" and passed into the great beyond.

I fought the long hair (I'll be honest, I'm still

not a fan). I scratched my head at the Tic-Tacs, baby dolls, and makeup fascination. But being the girly girl I am, I figured I could embrace the teeny tiny bit of femininity in my house, even if I know it's fleeting and merely curiosity. So, I sat with my boy and let him put makeup on me. I returned the favor, which, once he turned and looked at himself in the mirror, made him burst into tears and cry, "Get it off, get it off!"

I took it off. Then I poured a glass of wine and thought about how boring it would be in our house if it was only full of trucks, Nerf guns, and farts.

I don't know what it all means. To be honest, I don't really care. Maybe one will grow up to be a nurse who cares for babies. Maybe one will be a makeup artist. Maybe one will invent some cool new Tic-Tac box. Who knows? I see people raise their brows, purse their lips, and shake their heads at some of the things my boys like/do/say. I get it, but I know we all have our quirks; those little things make us individuals. Remember the tiara I wore to walk the dog? Sometimes I wear it to clean house—it makes me feel pretty. My boys may not fit into what people think of as the typical boy mold, and that's okay. As long as they're kind, healthy, and happy, I embrace all the quirks.

My kids each bring something different to the

table, and while I don't always understand or like it (the grossness of watching your son try and eat spaghetti, while his hair mixes with the sauce and then goes into his mouth, is sometimes too much), I won't fight it. They're exploring, trying to find their place in this crazy and sometimes messed-up world, so I'll sit back, sip my wine, and watch with wonder.

My son could compete in Olympic distance running.
For his stories.
His mouth just goes, and goes, and goes . . .

Chapter 8

If the Olympics Featured Little Kids

When the Olympics were happening one summer, I was watching with my husband and the water polo event came on. I have to admit I'd never watched water polo before. When they got into the pool, I just assumed they were doing distance swimming. I looked up from cutting vegetables to see two of the team members hugging.

"Why are they hugging?" I asked my husband.

"They're not. They're trying to dunk each other under the water."

"Why is that even allowed, and why is no one stopping the fight?"

My husband realized at that moment I had no clue what I was watching, and hence explained water polo to me. I sat, mesmerized, because I thought this was truly the funniest sport I had ever seen. Little capped heads bobbing in the water, doing a funny body shimmy to rise up out of the water and throw the ball, the splashing each other, and of course, the hugging. It reminded me of watching my boys play at the pool.

It was then that I started envisioning what the Olympics would be like if it was comprised of little kids.

Little Kid Olympics

Water Polo:

There would be the usual body shimmy in the water, like a dolphin bobbing for its food, but mostly you would see the kids going under the water, nothing happening, and then hearing the whole team shouting, "Watch this! Hey, watch this." You'd watch, waiting for something amazing (or anything really) to happen. Nothing would happen. All of this would be complete with colored floaties.

There would also be the kid who shouts, "Look, Mom, I'm making my own bubbles!"

And finally, lots of sideline goggle adjusting.

Long-Distance Running:

This would start off great, but about halfway

around the track, you'd see at least one kid sitting on the track crying because "She was running faster than me!" or "The ground is too haaaard!" There would be the kid who sees his mom in the stands and starts running like a deranged chicken, side to side, silly grin on his face, trying to stick his butt out and yelling, "Ha! Mom, I farted." (That would be my kid.)

At least three of the kids would simply stop running, because either the track is too long, it's too hot, the ground is too bumpy, or it's too sunshiney. The event would finally be cancelled because no one actually crossed the finish line.

Gymnastics:

This would be a fun one to watch with little kids, but only for a few minutes.

The bars would be a never-ending series of swings back and forth, complete with monkey sounds, until we heard, "Owww, my hands hurt." Most kids on the mat would spend their time trying to perfect a somersault, sideways of course. At least one kid would try to ride the balance beam like a horse, yelling, "Giddy up, giddy up. Hey, Mommy, look! I'm riding!" (This, too, would be my kid.)

There'd be one kid who would attempt to walk gracefully across the beam, but then the dismount would be a jump as far as possible, ending with a sprained ankle.

Ice Skating:

Kids on ice skates. Is there really anything more to describe?

A series of kids, arms outstretched, legs in a wide V, staying upright for all of 14 seconds before falling and saying, "I hate ice skating!"

Bike Racing:

This would entail a bunch of kids on bikes—with training wheels—constantly looking behind themselves, asking, "Are you holding on, Mommy? Mommy, don't let go." No one would finish, because the parents would get too tired from running behind them "holding on."

Soccer:

This one might work out okay. Kids, plus running, plus a ball is usually a good combo. The game would inevitably be thrown, because there's that one kid who is consistently making goals into the opposing team's net (yes, my kid). It would be too hard to keep score.

Thankfully, the Olympic competitors are adults who can run even when it's too sunshiney, manage to adjust their own goggles, and hold their gas until after the event (I hope). But if there ever is an Olympic sport of video gaming, farting on competitors (or siblings') heads, potato chip eating, or running into walls, I have two boys who would for sure take home the gold.

I could tolerate Monday better if it happened every Friday.

Chapter 9

It Started Young

I mentioned in the Introduction that my eldest, Aidan, has ADHD. Traveling the ADHD road has been tough. There is still a stigma surrounding the diagnosis, with some people claiming it isn't even a real thing. There are those who say it's lazy parenting, lack of discipline, food issues, and on and on. I am not going to try and educate anyone on ADHD; I've already spent too many hours doing that. I am simply going to describe my experience with my son, in the hopes that parents out there dealing with the same thing might find solace in the fact that they're not alone. It is real in my world and it is hard. I salute every parent who has to manage this and make some hard decisions.

Aidan was always an active kid. Like, really active. I remember when he was only about 18 months old and my parents would come over to visit—all he wanted to do was dance. We'd turn on the music, crank it up, and dance with him. My parents would do the best they could to keep up, but they pretty much only lasted one song and had to take a rest. Aidan would stop his dancing and walk over to them, grabbing their hands and saying, "More, Mema. Come, more."

He hated wearing pants (a child after my own heart), so usually if he was at home, he was just in his diaper. Unless it was Naked Time, when we would let him roam diaper-less, to help with his sensitive skin/diaper rash issue. This was always a gamble with an un-potty-trained kid, so we did this until the day he was sitting in his Tigger chair and peed all over it. It was his favorite chair, and he sobbed at the thought of us having to throw it out. I washed it as best I could, but it had a funk after that and didn't sit flat anymore, so I finally tossed it one day and surprised him with a Winnie the Pooh chair. The joke became: we threw out the Pee chair and bought him a Pooh one instead.

Anyhow, back to the activity tornado that was my son. Because his dad and I both worked, we had to put Aidan in daycare from a young age. He adapted well and we were lucky to find (mostly) nice people to care for him. Aidan was a super cute little guy, so teachers always took to him. My child has always smiled more than he's cried, always been happy, always liked to make others laugh, and always had a question for anyone who would listen. Actually, he didn't even care if you were listening. He talked anyway. Always. Teachers liked him but they often couldn't handle him in a classroom setting, because he was always moving, talking, singing, humming, dancing—anything that involved movement and being active.

Being an only child (and a girl), I assumed this was just boys. You always hear how active they are, but the teachers would pull me aside on pick-up and talk to me about Aidan.

"He has trouble keeping his hands to himself."

"He wouldn't lie down for his nap today."

"He sang the whole nap time."

"He wouldn't sit still for art time."

It seemed endless. I didn't know what to do since none of those things seemed that bad to me. I would talk to him about keeping his hands to himself, being still and quiet during nap, and so on. But it didn't change.

Again, it didn't seem that bad, because he was my son and I loved him. I, too, would get frustrated, because it never seemed like I could get him to do what I needed him to when I needed him to, but I figured this was just him being a kid. For example, I'd tell him in the morning to put his clothes on.

I'd go grab my bag and when I came back, he'd be playing with a toy. If I asked him to go get his shoes, he would come back with a book instead, asking me to read it to him (not that he would sit still for that). Dinners took forever, because he would talk and play with his food for an hour. He never liked to sit and play with toys much, although he loved it when I would make voices for his animals and toys, and we would converse. Getting him to color was impossible. He'd pick one color, scribble on the page, then ask to do something else. Play-Doh was a bit better, but that usually lasted only a few minutes tops. He never wanted to sit and look at books, unless it was time to read before bed. I tried painting with him, doing crafts, baking, but nothing held his attention for more than a few minutes before he was on to the next thing. It became normal for me. This was my son.

Then he started kindergarten and that's when everything changed. The emails from the teacher seemed to come daily about him not focusing, disrupting class, doing silly things. He'd sit for an entire lesson and just play with his pencil, doodling instead of writing down answers.

In first grade, he was finally diagnosed with

ADHD, and while that made everything make sense, it didn't make school any easier.

And so began the hell that was school for us. Here are just a few of the emails I have received over the years about Aidan in school:

Preschool

Hi Heather,

Today Aidan kept getting in Hunter's face and opening and closing his mouth like a fish out of water. He also wouldn't sit still in art and kept getting up, saying he must have ants in his pants. Then he pulled his pants down to look.

Thank you,

Miss M.

Kindergarten

Hi Heather,

Today Aidan missed recess because he was burping in a classmate's face. When I asked why he did it, he said, "I didn't burp IN her face. I was burping and her face got in the way." I have to admit I chuckled some because I wasn't expecting that, but please remind Aidan tonight that it is not polite to burp at school or in his classmate's face.

Thank you,
Mrs. A

1st Grade

Hi Heather,

Today has been a little rocky. He's having definite focus issues, but the biggest thing is he has been going around calling people in class "sexy." Not sure where this came from. He says he doesn't know what it means, but he did say he knew it was not an appropriate word for school. I'll let you handle this one. Needless to say, it definitely made me giggle when I heard what the word was. :)

Thank you,
Mrs. L

(at least she had a sense of humor)

2nd Grade

Hi,

Aidan has a behavior slip in his backpack that needs to be signed. He was caught today by a second-grade teacher, climbing on the toilets in the bathroom and peeking under the stalls. He missed first recess to fill out the behavior slip and had to make two color changes. The rest of the day after this incident went much better, though. Let me know if you have any questions or concerns.

Thanks much,
Mrs. K

Hi again,

Just thought I'd drop a quick note. I have been noticing changes over the last week in Aidan's behavior and focus and wondering if you had noticed the same. Today, he has really been struggling with not just focusing on work, but to the point of disrupting the whole class. His explanation was that he didn't have enough breakfast*. Thought you would want to know.

Thanks.

*My kid ate like a horse every morning. Usually oatmeal, yogurt, and some fruit. Sigh.

6th Grade

Hello,

I wanted to let you know that Aidan refused to do work today in 5th period, so he does have homework. During the warm-up activity the prompt was, 'If you could be any character from a movie or book, who would you be and why?' They had five minutes to write and Aidan wrote, 'I want to be Godzilla.' That was it. Please have him write more at home.

Have a nice day,

Mrs. T

There are more, but I'm sure you get the idea by now. School meant torture for all of us, and it was all I could do to not take my boys, move to a farm out in the middle of nowhere, and live the simple life. But, my husband reminded me, there are no malls and I would have to drive forever to meet any other women, so I stayed put.

My son gave me a foot rub last night. It was the best 2.34 seconds of my life.

Chapter 10

My Wish for You

So yes, my son has ADHD and I have wine.

But seriously, I live and breathe ADHD in all its noisy, moving, shaking, singing, obsessing, avoiding, forgetting glory. I write about it a lot, and I research it almost daily, trying to find new studies, anything that might help Aidan.

I'm going to be honest, I hate it. I hate that he has it, I hate that his life is most likely going to be harder than most because of it, and I hate that I can't do more for him. I'm the "control mom" who would follow him around and remind him of everything he's forgetting, but thankfully I'm a tad smarter than that and realize I would someday like to experience the heartbreak of the "empty-nest" syndrome. I might also like grandkids—but one of these boys better produce a female!

The world can be cruel and people can be mean. Not everyone understands Aidan or ADHD, and not everyone cares to take the time to try. I'm more afraid for his future than his brother's or stepbrother's—boys who can sit still in class and remember their homework (and underwear). Boys who pick up on social cues and know when to stop trying so hard, who know when to quiet down or back off. I hate the ADHD.

But I don't hate *him*, of course. I just hate that it makes everyone's life a little harder. I ache for him when I see him struggle in school, forget an assignment, or realize that he has failed at being "normal"—again. That's why I wanted to write down everything I hope for him in life. He won't read this anytime soon (since reading is tantamount to climbing a mountain for him), but someday he'll be able to see this and know how much I want for him. I may have failed on the daily journal, but I *am* getting some things down!

Everything I Wish for You, Aidan

1. Never give up your silly side just to fit in. I want you to be confident enough to continue to dance like a deranged chicken, and to sing loudly

and laugh, even when you know you have the words wrong.

2. Never stop doodling—even if it is in school. I love the wonderful pictures you create in the margins of your notebook, even if there are more pictures than words. I'd rather look at that talent than read an essay I know was torture for you to get down on paper, because you had to sit and focus for 45 minutes to get just one paragraph done.

3. I hope you never lose your empathy for others. You and Gavin fight like the Japanese army fought Godzilla, but if Gavin is in harm's way, there is no better protector on this planet than you. If someone is being made fun of, you are the kid who will befriend the underdog and try to make him feel better. You're the one who will use your own money to buy extra sour candies to share with your friends, not to get them to like you, but because sharing makes you happy.

4. I hope you never lose your ability to always look at the bright side of life, to rarely let this chaotic and often cruel world get you down. To continue trying to get others to look at the bright side too. "You should relax more, Mom," you tell me. "You look prettier when you smile."

5. Always challenge the "norm," whether it's

refusing to wear matching socks (because that's boring), to writing your English paper on how the song "Pink Fluffy Unicorns Dancing on Rainbows" makes you happy.

6. I truly hope you find a woman to love you for your grandness. For the way you think, "This is fun! Let's make it even better!" For the way you smile, lopsided and big, when you're teasing. For the way you unexpectedly say the sweetest things like, "You smell like love." I hope she understands and embraces a life of messiness, of everything that is the opposite of normalcy. I hope she never loses sight of all the positives—the joy, the unwavering love, the committed-ness to making everything just a little bit bigger and better.

7. I hope you know how much you're loved. I'm not always the best parent, not always calm in the face of nonstop singing and fidgeting. Not always understanding about the messy room (usually within 10 minutes of my cleaning it), and I don't always say the right thing at the right time. But I love you. I love your smile, your heart, your unconventional ways. You make me laugh, you make me feel, you make me think. You have changed my life for the better in so many ways. I want you to always know how completely you own my heart.

8. Most of all, I want you to be happy. More

than anything. And in writing this, if you, my son, have taught me anything, it's that happiness comes with letting go a little of routines, of what is "normal" and what "should" be done. Easing up and simply enjoying the moment. And smiling, because we all look prettier when we smile.

Nothing makes me feel more beautiful than when my son says, "Oh, I love how squishy everything is on you."
Squishy.

Chapter 11

What Aidan Wants Grown-Ups to Know

I won't say I have never wondered about what life is like inside Aidan's head, because I do that almost daily. But I'd never really sat down and talked with him about it, mainly because getting him to sit and have a heart-to-heart is nearly impossible.

But one day we were chatting while I was making school lunches, and he started opening up about what it's like in his world. I put together what he said that day, along with other nuggets of insight he had previously dropped on me, and I wrote it all down that afternoon. When I was done and I reread all the things I had heard my boy say to me at different times, I was a crumpled heap of soggy tears with a fragile heart.

I was ashamed of myself for not listening closer each time he let me into his world. I was sad thinking about what it must be like for him, dealing with the knowledge that he's different because people tell him he is, but *feeling* like he is simply *him*. He's just Aidan, and being Aidan is all he knows how to be.

Our conversation that morning started out simple enough, about a girl he likes in school.

"She's the most popular girl, but some people say really mean things about her."

"What do they say that's mean?" I asked.

"They call her fat and say she's ugly without any makeup."

God, kids can be mean. I asked him how he felt when he heard people saying things like that.

"It makes me feel bad for her, because I know how I feel when people say mean things about me."

My mom radar went off. My son is that kid who is always happy; nothing seems to get him down. But he did not seem happy right now.

"What do you think people say?" I asked, expecting him to shrug and say, "I don't know." I got this instead:

I hear them, everything they probably think I can't hear. Like the sigh when I tell them I forgot my homework again. I hear them mutter things under their breath when I'm fidgeting in class. I hear frustration in their voices. I'd like them to understand I'm not trying to make them mad.

I see things too. Like how you smile less with me than with other kids. I see how Daddy's forehead gets all creased when he's yelling at me. I see people roll their eyes when I show them a new toy, and how they sound all mad when they ask me to stop singing.

I want people to know I feel like they don't like how I am. I want Daddy to know I'm not stupid and it hurts my feelings when he asks, "Are you dumb?" I want you to know I don't like it when you yell. I hate when I ask someone a question and they say, "It's none of your business. Stop interrupting." I'm just curious.

I just want it to stop—the yelling, comparing me to other kids who are "normal." How people tense up sometimes when I just walk into the room. I want people to say I'm nice and funny and good at drawing, and not follow it with, "If only he could focus like that in other areas." I just want to feel like it's okay to be me.

Holy shit! That was not what I expected. It took every ounce of strength I had not to crumble under the weight of my shame. Maybe my happy kid wasn't as happy as I thought. And I'd been so frustrated with him for not being "normal," I'd missed it.

It's a good parent teacher conference when I hear, "He's getting better at holding his gas until he gets to the bathroom."

Chapter 12

The Power of My Words

It was a day that seemed like any other. I woke and went through my normal routine—breakfast, packing lunches, yelling about getting socks on and to stop hitting each other—a day where everything seemed normal. Until it wasn't.

Aidan had been asking me all morning to come watch a video with him. He'd been talking about these videos all weekend, and I had dutifully nodded and murmured during his ramblings, saying multiple times, "Not right now."

I had just said no again as I put the dog in his kennel and pondered my to-do list when I looked up to see him standing there. His hands were twisting around one another, his shoulders slumped. He stared at me, frowning. I didn't understand what was happening and was about to give him grief for standing there with no socks on and not getting his bag together, but there was something about the way he looked that stopped me.

"What's wrong?" I asked.

"You just said you don't care," he said to me.

My first response was to quickly say, "No, I didn't," and move on. But my stomach clenched up. I felt something coming and I was nervous.

"Why are you standing there like that?" I asked, almost not wanting to hear the answer.

He shook his head, pulled his eyes away from mine, and went to put his socks on. Motherhood pushed me forward gently.

"Why were you just standing there looking at me like that?" I asked, bending down to look him in the eye, my hand on his knee.

I felt it before I saw it, that gut-wrenching feeling as you watch someone you love deeply hurting. He crumpled.

He wouldn't meet my eyes but I could see the tears in his. "It doesn't matter," he said.

But I heard him. It *did* matter. I didn't know what "it" was, but it mattered.

"Please talk to me," I said softly, still close to him.

"You just said you don't care," he said, struggling to hold back tears. "I asked you to come watch the video, and you said no and you don't care."

That was the moment I realized that what I say is not always what he hears.

My son is and always has been a very *feeling* boy. He is so in tune with my moods and emotions that he can tell when I have a migraine, when I'm tired, when I'm stressed, and when I'm happy without my saying a word. He knows that when my left eye droops, it's a bad headache. He knows that when I'm pale, I'm tired. He knows that when I sigh deeply, I'm stressed and thinking about something. Likewise, I believe this little person sitting in front of me is someone I know better than anybody or anything. I know his voice, his musty pre-teen smell, the way the right side of his hair curls up in the front when it gets too long. I know his sense of humor, his hobbies, his struggles. I know.

But it hit me in that moment that my son might know *me* better than I know *him*.

And when it hits me that there's something I don't know, I'm stunned.

I don't know how my son sees his world. His world is not like mine. Hell, it's not like a lot of people's. It's not what most would call "normal." He lives in his ADHD world, which is so different from mine that we might as well be on different planets, speaking different languages.

In fact, sometimes I think maybe we *do* speak different languages. Because my son is noisy, continually moving, forgetful, persistent to a fault, eager, excitable, messy, and more, his days are filled with people telling him to stop. Stop talking, humming, doodling, moving. Stop and clean up your mess, do your homework, and remember your socks. Stop asking questions, stop fidgeting—just stop. It gets tiresome, so tiresome, even for me and I'm his mother. I can only imagine how his teachers, friends, brother, stepbrother, stepparents, and grandparents feel. They're not tied to him like I am with my fierce Momma Bear feeling that wants to protect him from everything: all the hurt, pain, and judgment that comes at him—daily—because he's different.

When I realized that I had become one of those people who discounts him, who just wants him to be . . . well, not like him, it crushed me. When he gets into something, he gets into it with all his being. The stuff he gets into is important to him, all-consuming at times, and because it's important to him, he wants to share that with the people he cares about. But because he ends up being so persistent, not knowing when to stop asking or take no for an answer, he ends up hurting. Because people get tired—tired of saying no, tired of him asking the same question eight different ways, hoping to get the answer he's looking for.

Our conversation made me see that he is so

used to hearing no, so used to being discounted, ignored, and getting people upset, that he hears everything through a lens of negativity. My simple no got translated into "I don't care about your video. I don't care about you." My actions were telling him everything else was more important.

I could have sat there and argued with him, explained why he was wrong, told him that's not what I said. But instead I said, "I'm sorry I hurt you. I do care. Right now, we need to get ready for school, but how about we plan to watch the video tonight after dinner?" That's all it took. He perked up and sat straighter and said, "You promise?" I nodded.

I do promise. I promise to keep kindness in mind. I promise to remember it only takes a second to hear someone and let them know they've been heard. This is vital for all my relationships, but even more so for my ADHD son, who lives in the *World of No.* I promise to work to change "no" to "not right now but how about later?" I can't always say yes and I won't, but I can be gentler in how I reply. I can work to ensure my words accurately reflect my intent. I don't always have to be interested in his stuff, but I can be interested in *him.*

I promise. I can listen. I care. It hurts how much I care.

My son had an "amazing" dream last night that he started telling me about at breakfast.

I'll let you know how it ends, once he's out of college and done telling me about it.

Chapter 13

My Biggest Lie

There came a day when the one thing I had worked so hard to avoid for Aidan became un-avoidable.

I held the little pills in my hand and I broke. I'd lost the fight and was now battling a new war. With his small, trusting face looking at me, I told the biggest lie of my life: "This is safe. You'll be fine. I promise." Everything in my being screamed at me, "Liar! Horrible mother! Failure!"

The first day I gave Aidan drugs for his ADHD was one of the hardest days of my life. I had fought against holding those pills in my palm for such a long time that finding myself in my kitchen with the bottle was surreal. I tried to console myself by saying I had done everything I could to not be in this position. The "natural approach," limiting food dyes, the expensive "natural light" bulbs in our kitchen, the mini trampoline. I remembered the laps run around our living room. I had fought a good fight for a long time.

To make this defeat even worse, Aidan didn't want to take the pills. Having a severe nut allergy, he was overly cautious about trying new foods. If it wasn't something he'd had before, he didn't want to try it. Whether it was a food, a restaurant, or even candy, if it was new, it wasn't going into his body. Getting him to swallow that pill was a battle of wills—one that I eventually won after tears (on both sides), promises, threats, and finally a bribe.

I'd told him it was safe, but I knew I shouldn't promise that. I'd read the research about the side effects and it scared me. The research was only about 20 years old and not done on my son. How could I know that he wouldn't be the one kid who'd have an adverse reaction? How could I know it wouldn't affect his brain's ability to form the way it should because I was pushing little pills into his body at a formative age? How would I know it would work? Yet, I promised him that I knew, and because I'm his mom, his protector, and the person who loves him more than anything, he believed me and swallowed the pill.

That day and the days that followed.

Opening that bottle each morning was a reminder that I was mothering blind. I watched him for signs of changes—in his mood, appetite, sleep, anything. He stopped eating lunch because he "just wasn't hungry." Teachers began to tell me he was calmer but *not* more focused. He could sit, but couldn't concentrate any better. He was not a disruption—most of the time.

I didn't give him the pills on the weekends because I hated seeing him calm. I know it sounds crazy, but my boy isn't supposed to be calm. He's vibrant, wild, loud, crazy, and at times (many, many times) makes me want to scream in frustration and tiredness. But *that* is my boy. That is how we roll. The quiet, calm kid who was now so skinny that his doctor said we needed to try and get him to eat more calories in any form was not my son. I couldn't bear the changes those pills made in him, so I only gave them to him on school days. Not on weekends. Not during the summer.

I continued with the pills for five years. Different pills at times, each one a promise to make things perfect.

Then he reached middle school and started being more vocal about not wanting to take the pills. "I want to WANT to eat lunch," he said. "I don't like how they make me feel."

I was now forcing my kid to take drugs, and he was begging me to stop.

Middle school was constant parent-teacher meetings, because he was *still* not doing his work. The daily emails stating he needed to do extra homework because he'd been staring off into space all day were overwhelming. I was breaking. He was too. The nightly fights about getting homework done were killing us. It was sucking the joy out of our relationship. His self-esteem was nil, my patience was long gone, and we were all suffering. And still, each day we woke, I handed him the pills and a lunchbox I knew would come home full. He took them, not meeting my eyes, his compliance saying more than his defiance ever could.

My failure and my shame made my skin tight, and my stomach unraveled. Each visit to the "specialist" to get his three-month prescription refilled (only three months because people use this drug to get high) was crushing. I kept hoping time would change things, that maybe a new drug could help. We tried four, each with its own hellish side effects. The mornings we'd start a new drug added more notches in my guilt belt.

"Are you SURE this one is okay?" he'd ask, still trusting me.

I would nod, the lies coming easier now. But the guilt was becoming harder to carry.

Things have changed for us due to a myriad

of reasons. He's maturing, we found an alternative school, where he can learn in ways that work best for HIM and at his own pace. But, the biggest change has been, he no longer swallows those pills. I no longer carry my cloak of guilt. I finally realized, things were ALREADY perfect. I have exactly the son I am supposed to have, perfect in his imperfection, as we all are.

I write this to those who think that WE, the parents who choose to medicate, do so easily. That we do so because we've been brainwashed or because we haven't "tried hard enough." Medicating your child is NOT an easy decision and I would be hard pressed to find a parent who didn't struggle with the decision. I write this as a window into this hell and as a request to PLEASE, be kinder to these parents who have had to make this horrible decision. For some, it is a life changer and the best decision ever. For others, like me, it helped some but was not the game changer I'd hoped. For some, it changes nothing and they are back to square one.

Be kind (in all ways), reserve judgment and may you never find yourself faced with a decision like this. One where you must make a promise to your child, that you are not sure you can keep.

Parenting is as easy as taking candy from a baby.
A baby T-Rex or rabid raccoon, that is.

Chapter 14

I Stopped Parenting the ADHD

I'd subconsciously resigned myself to mothering the ADHD more than my son, meaning I was spending most of my time trying to combat the ADHD and forgetting about the boy within. I would have flashes of insight, where I remembered the human being inside the ADHD diagnosis, and I would feel such shame that I had let the daily grind of missing homework, forgotten socks, lost papers, and loud noises take center stage. I would cringe with regret once my boys were asleep, knowing I'd once again let my frustration get the better of me and that I'd spent the evening yelling—the thing my son has told me he hates the most—because sometimes, the yelling seemed to be the only thing that made the madness stop.

Now I'm here on the cusp of my son turning 14. I look back and don't recognize that woman or that little boy. There were times I was sure he would grow to hate me, because I couldn't keep my emotions in check. Because I broke down and let exhaustion win. Times when I would admit I didn't know what to do anymore, and that he just *had* to learn how to assimilate better into the world I was used to living in. My biggest fear was that he would grow to say he never felt loved, never felt close to me, and that he remembers me always being angry.

I was angry a lot.

Recently, it was just the two of us at home and we were being silly, laughing about something. It was the kind of deep belly laugh that for a moment steals your breath and fills you with joy, until you regain your air and it comes out in a laugh that shakes your core. He looked at me and said, "Seeing you happy is the best thing in my life."

Those words entered me and burrowed so deeply into my core that I stopped to take a deep breath to make room for them. It hit me then: We were on the other side of ADHD. I'm not saying my son no longer exhibits ADHD symptoms. He does. But unless he's rocking back and forth and slapping the armrest on an airplane (recent happening), or singing the same line of a song over and over and over and over, ADHD hardly has a home with us anymore.

Why?

I believe it was because we switched schools, and at the same time, my son stopped taking the ADHD meds. I credit this private school, a school full of kids who have been labeled "different, challenged, deficient, and even defiant at times" with saving my son. And me. This school is full of teachers who *get* these kids, who teach them in super small classes or one on one, so that each child learns in the way that suits him or her best. For example, my son got to do a report on the planets based on characters from his favorite video game. He had to research the planets' atmospheres and figure out which character could live on which planet. He worked with a friend to put together a PowerPoint presentation. He talked about that presentation for weeks and was beside himself with pride the day he presented it to me and his dad.

Because my son got to the point where he was hating the ADHD medication and it was becoming a daily argument about why he had to take it, I said we would try this new school with no meds and see how things worked out. He has been off meds for over a year now. Are things perfect? Nope. He still struggles in a class setting, even if it's only with a few other kids, so he does most of his classes one on one. But, he's learning. He's happy to go to school, and when he recently tried to tell me who his favorite teachers were, he got so flustered that he stopped and said, "I can't do this. I like all my teachers. They're all nice people and good teachers."

Finding a place for him to fit in, a place where he feels safe, respected, listened to, and *capable,* has made all the difference. I know not everyone has a private school like this near them, and if they do, cost might be an issue. I'm not writing this to say all ADHD kids need to go to private school, but this has proven that at least in my son's case, many of *our* issues were based on the stress of trying to get him to fit into a typical public school. We're not perfect, but we're so much better.

Now that we have this stress off our shoulders, we get to enjoy each other. We laugh more, we talk about things other than school, and I feel closer to him than I ever have. He's turning into a young man, one who fills me with pride when I see his compassion, his sense of humor, his desire to make others happy. A young man who is growing into an adult way too quickly, but an adult who I am positive will find his way in the world. An adult who will enrich the lives of those who are fortunate enough to cross paths with him. He'll have struggles—we all do—but I finally believe he will be okay.

I'm working to ensure he has more memories of seeing me happy than seeing me angry. I'm not claiming perfection yet, but I'm enjoying parenting more because now, I parent my son and not the ADHD.

I'm at my most sarcastic when I'm awake.

Chapter 15

Hello, Little Son, I've Missed You

I've written a lot about Aidan and his ADHD, both in this book and on my Facebook page and Twitter, and in personal journals. My friends and family ask how things are with the boys, and I always start off with what is happening with Aidan. Sometimes, it's as though Gavin has been lost in the craziness. He's here—I care for him, talk with him, and make sure he knows he's loved and taken care of, but in dealing with life, Aidan, step-parenting, and divorced parenting, I often forget Gavin needs me too.

Little Son,

I'm sorry. I've missed you. I'm sorry about how often you must yell even louder than your brother in order to be heard. And then, because you're being so loud, I yell at you in frustration to stop. Because with Aidan around, it is already so loud and chaotic that when you chime in, my world goes dark and I need it to stop. I'm sorry that Aidan is the one I talk about most with friends and family and that you most likely hear that. Granted, the talk is usually about how frustrated/ worried/stressed/overwhelmed I am, but I doubt that matters much in your young world.

I'm so sorry that homework time usually ends up with you doing yours on your own, while I wrestle, cajole, and spend my evening trying to help Aidan. You sit like a little champ and do your math problems, reading, and spelling review. Yet I don't often take the time to praise you for what a good job you do, because I am so worried that Aidan will hear and feel bad about himself. I let my fear of his reaction keep me from gushing about your greatness.

I feel so guilty about how often you have to endure my bad moods in the mornings because I'm at my wit's end trying to get Aidan out the door. You go upstairs, get dressed (with socks AND clean underwear!), brush your teeth, and try to brush your hair. I come *up and see Aidan playing with the dog, wearing only dirty underwear, no socks, and the mask from his Halloween costume, and I yell. You look at me with your big blue eyes, and I can see that you've noticed. You've noticed that I didn't notice you. You see that once again, my focus is on Aidan.*

I'm sorry Aidan is so mean to you. I wish I could explain the sibling thing, but being an only child, I'm at a loss. I am told the fighting is normal, but I see how much you adore your brother and how, when he's mean to you, your little face falls, your eyes look down, and you deflate a little. You're not stupid. In fact, you're super smart. I think you're amazing. But I don't say that because I worry Aidan will think I'm comparing you two and see the comparison is unequal, tipped greatly to your side. He might feel worse about himself, and that might make things even worse for you. I try hard not to compare you two, because I know you are different people, with different personalities, struggles, and strengths. But in my failure to compare, I haven't given you the praise and attention you need, that you deserve.

But I think the time has come for me to realize it is not all about Aidan. You need me too. You need validation, praise, rewards, and thank yous, independent of Aidan—and you need them whether he gets them or not. You need to know how amazing you are, how kind, funny, and wicked smart. You're in 2nd grade and reading and doing math at a 3rd-grade level. You're so flipping coordinated in basketball (and most sports for that matter) that I am blown away when I watch you. My heart aches when I tell you how talented you are and you look sad and say, "I'm not any good."

YOU ARE GOOD! In fact, you are more than good: You are amazing. And while I have said my goal is to help Aidan navigate his way through a non-ADHD world, it's also helping you navigate your world too. I want you to feel seen, heard, and proud of everything you bring to this world. Because you bring a ton, Little Son.

There will be no more shadow for you to get lost behind. I want the light to shine on your wonder, your greatness, your beautiful strawberry hair and gorgeous blue eyes. I want you to know and feel this light. You'll never walk in the shadows again.

I love you,
Mom

They say it's important to keep things fun in a marriage.
I like to randomly greet my husband at the door and ask, "Notice anything different?"
There's nothing different.

Chapter 16

The Unconscious Uncoupling and the Conscious Coupling (and Now I Need a Drink)

Okay, I'm going to be honest and admit I never read any of the stories on exactly what Gwyneth Paltrow and Chris Martin were doing when they had their "Conscious Uncoupling." (If you don't know them, they're super famous people who married, then divorced in a "Conscious Uncoupling" way. Also, they're too pretty to be real.) I imagine it meant they were fully mentally present through thehellthatisdivorce, and did so with open minds, open hearts, and pure joy.

Whatever.

I took part in UNconscious uncoupling, which in my book meant everything was a colossal mess, my brain was fried from stress, lack of sleep, regret, anger, shame, and pain, and everything basically sucked ass. I won't go into everything that led up to my uncoupling except to say that I wouldn't wish it on anyone. The worst part was that I was thinner than ever and couldn't even enjoy it because, well, we were uncoupling!

Okay, that was a horrendous time, and while I don't kid myself that it was easy for my boys, I do applaud myself and my ex for keeping it civil for their sake. We're not perfect, but I have heard and seen true horror stories of putting the kids in the middle, and I can go to my grave knowing neither of us did that. I feel truly proud of myself and grateful to my ex for that.

Fast forward to now and I am happier than I ever dreamed with my new husband. He brought with him a son from his previous marriage, and so the house of three boys, one man, and a male dog was formed. Oh, and me, the poor girly girl, who really does own three tiaras and lives for the holiday collections from MAC cosmetics.

Blending our families has been magical. Our kids met and all fell in love (more brothers, yay!) and never fight. They are kind to each other and have the best time playing outside, running and laughing until they're so exhausted from all the fun, they collapse into bed. They each try to outdo the other with how helpful they are around the house, and it is not uncommon for me to hear, "I'm done with the dishes. Can I have a turn at vacuuming now?"

Okay, I may be exaggerating a bit.

A mom can dream, can't she?

Here's the more realistic version:

Blending families pretty much sucks. We have my two boys who like to spend their free time fighting over things, like who was breathing louder or whose name is first on Santa's nice list. The irony is not lost on me. They're used to having to share (not always gratefully), not having a lot of privacy ("Hey Gavin, are you done pooping? No? Okay, I'll sit with you and we'll watch this funny video. Wow, you stink."), and our house being LOUD.

Then we have my stepson. He is an only child who's used to entertaining himself and pooping alone. When it was just him and his dad, the main sound in the house was the TV or his video game. His toys are all his, and there is no one to tell him that no, the best way to eat soup is not with a spoon but with a straw because . . . well . . . it just IS! The poor kid is outnumbered, outshouted, and at times, exhausted.

The one saving grace has been how relaxed and laid back I am about how my husband parents his son. Because we have decidedly different parenting styles (Mars and Venus and all that), it would be easy for me to sit and be judgmental about his choices—which differ greatly from mine—on everything from foods, screen time, and bedtime, to clothing, dealing with attitude, and instilling responsibility. Thankfully, I am mature enough to understand that we are different, and that no one has the complete playbook on proper parenting, least of all me. So, I embrace our differences and allow him to be the father he needs to be.

Aahahaha!

You almost bought that didn't you?

Well, I can say this: I am getting better and a little less bitchy. It's a 142-step process, folks, and I'm only on step six. But I'm working on taming my own monkeys and wrangling my own circus, because Lord knows there's plenty for me to do there. And that is one of the many reasons why we joined a few wine clubs and I installed a lock on the closet door.

Priorities.

I'm at my most optimistic when I only grab a hand basket at the grocery store.

Chapter 17

Sometimes, I'm Not Very Nice to Me

Many times, when I'm feeling overwhelmed, I will sit down and write a letter to whomever is on my mind, telling them how I'm feeling. I've written to my boys, my husband, my ex, my mom, friends, etc. I even wrote to Oprah once, because I really wanted to be on her Favorite Things show. She didn't reply.

But recently I was finding myself very angry at me. The voice in my head (just one voice that day) was being a complete and total bitch! I thought I couldn't do anything right, and I made sure to keep a rolling dialogue going for most of the day about how I was failing. That night, after the boys were down, I sat in a hot bath and cried.

I felt the need to write, but this time I wrote to me. What would I say to a good friend who was dealing with everything I was and talking about herself the way I was? I kinda wanted to kick my own ass, but instead I wrote this:

Dear Me,

I'm not sure where to start, but it feels like a heartfelt "I'm sorry" would be good. I've been thinking about you a lot lately, and I feel ashamed for the way I've treated you. While I know better than anyone how hard things are at times, I've still constantly sat in judgment of you.

I'm so sorry.

I live your daily struggle with Aidan. I see how hard you work to help him manage his ADHD and processing disorder. I know you spend countless hours researching, reading, trying new things, and worrying. But I still chime in each day, telling you how you've not done enough, and how you yelled this morning, which you KNOW is the worst possible way to communicate with your ADHD child. I remind you the laundry is still not folded, and that you ordered pizza when you had perfectly good chicken sitting in the fridge. I tell you these are the actions of a mom who is NOT doing her job right. I tell you this is

what lazy moms do, moms who don't care.
I'm sorry.

Last week you spent time volunteering at Aidan's school and filling out the eight-foot pile of back-to-school forms. You bought school supplies and new clothes, and you got all of Aidan's medical forms filled out and signed by the doc so his medicines would be approved for school. But, at the end of the week, I chastised you for being too tired to work out (your pants are getting snug) and forgetting to make an appointment with the allergist. I'm sorry.

On Saturday, after you'd taken all three boys to the trampoline house, to the store for a treat (probably not the best idea—sugar is the devil), then cooked dinner and finally got the laundry done, I made you feel bad for not watching that mind-numbing cartoon when Gavin asked and for having that second glass of wine. I'm sorry.

And those are just the recent things I'm sorry for. I think back on the years of us being a mom, and I cringe at how I've treated you. I'm also sorry for making you feel shame when you had to go to work every day and drop Aidan at daycare when he was little. I know you needed to work, but I still made you feel horrible. I told you all the other moms were judging you for not making it to every class party, field trip, or concert. I sat in judgment of you when Aidan's dad had to work late and you let him zone out in front of the television (screen time will rot his brain, I said), while you cooked and cleaned up. I'm sorry.

When your marriage crumbled and you were a shattered shell of a human, I said you were ruining your children's lives by being selfish and wanting out. I told you they would someday hate you. I told you everyone you know would judge you too. I watched you stay for a year and a half and struggle. I watched you lose yourself and I judged you. I shamed you. I'm sorry.

Each time you've allowed yourself to be even a little bit human, to feel overwhelmed with the day, the noise, the fighting, the pee on the floor, the messy rooms, the refusal to eat the healthy dinner you cooked, I judged you. I reminded you that YOU chose to have kids, and I said you needed to step up and overcome those feelings. I told you other moms did it and I shamed you with, "Why can't you?" I chastised you for not being perfect, for being human. I'm sorry.

I want to change for you. I want to support you in this crazy, joyous, scary, and oftentimes overwhelming journey. I want to be your biggest cheerleader when you're successful (Aidan finally puts new underwear on each day—yay!) and your safety net on those dark days, when it all feels like it's too much and you're not sure how you'll cope with one more school detention for missing homework. I want you to end each day hearing me say, "You did the best you could today. You're awesome!" I want you to know that I mean it. Because I KNOW how hard you try. I KNOW how deeply you love. I KNOW how difficult it can be.

So, my dearest me, I'm sorry for the past. I am committed to you, to our journey through motherhood, and to supporting you in being the best possible mom and human you can be.

You're awesome! And you're pretty!

This letter totally made me feel better that night, and there are still times I open this up on my computer after a particularly hard day and reread it. It doesn't fix anything, but it reminds me that I'm human, I'm doing my best, and that I need to cut myself some slack for that third glass of wine.

My son said he can't wait to be an adult so he can do what he wants, when he wants.
I laughed so hard I spit my wine on the 10-foot pile of laundry I was folding.

Chapter 18

Sometimes I Hide

Sometimes I hide in my closet. I know, this seems to be the "mommy" thing to do these days—drink wine, hide in closets, and cry. But I was hiding in my closet before it became the cool thing to do.

The first time I hid was because of a particularly rough day in Mom-land. I needed space, I needed air, and I needed to be alone. I cleared a space between my shirts and sat. I was quiet. Gavin was crying in his room and Aidan was yelling at him.

I closed my eyes and envisioned the beach. *A beach with a crying child.* No, wait, that's not right. I tried it again. *A beach with only the waves and wind.*

"Mommy??" a frantic wave said. A wave? Ugh, it's Aidan.

"Mommy, where are you?" The panic in his voice made him sound younger than his 12 years.

I said nothing. I kept my eyes closed and watched the waves. I breathed deeply.

"Moooommmmmmeeeeee!" He was getting closer; it sounded like he was in my room. I only had seconds left, so I put my toe in the water and felt the waves caress my feet.

"What are you doing?"

He'd found me.

"I'm breathing and enjoying the waves," I said, opening my eyes. He was staring at me. I knew he was confused. So was I. How had being a mother become so hard? How had I become so out of my element, so out of my mind, and so out of patience that I was curled up between my shirts on the floor of my closet envisioning talking waves, while my kids played a game of hide-and-seek where no one knew the rules?

He looked at me expectantly.

I would have an answer. I always did. Right?

I had no answer.

I had no energy left to answer even if there had been one.

"Are you okay?" he asked. "Why are you on the floor of your closet?"

I wanted to tell him the truth—that they had reduced me to this. Their fighting, their constant need, his inability to complete the tasks I asked of him, his constant singing. All of this had sapped me of my strength, and the only place left that felt safe was the dark corner of my closet surrounded by my clothes that smelled clean. I opened my mouth to speak but nothing came out. I was like a fish gasping for air. I felt horrible.

I'm not sure how life turned into this. When I look back 10 years ago, if you'd told me this was how life would be, I would have died laughing. In some ways it is exponentially better, and in others, well, it leaves me sitting in the corner of my closet.

It's amazing as a mom, because I can feel this way—like there is no hope and I will never be able to stand again, or cook them dinner, or referee another fight—and then something kicks in and I do stand. I don't want to but I do. I stand and I walk out and I do what I need to do. Everything is heavy and I want nothing more than to sleep, but instead I cook, I referee, and I bathe and read a bedtime book. I do it all without complaining, and they are none the wiser.

Deep down I know I'm normal. I know this is not easy—not just motherhood but life in general. There's so much pressure to be perfect, to do it all and do it well (hello, Pinterest. I'm looking at you here). I want you each to know that at night, after the kids are down and the house is quiet, it is completely normal to stuff an entire red velvet cupcake into your mouth, then wash it down with a Diet Coke and tell yourself they cancel each other out.

You are not alone.

"I think you have poop on your cheek."

-Things I never thought I'd say.

Chapter 19

They Say It Takes a Village.

I Don't Have a Village.

Where the Fuck Is My Village??

There seems to be a vanishing happening in my life lately. I often remind myself of the wise African proverb, "It takes a village to raise a child." I repeat this when I'm late getting my boys to school in the mornings, or when we're arguing in the checkout line because they just have to have the gum/candy/shitty-toy hanging in their faces. I repeat it when we're doing the bedtime routine, which usually ends with mommy yelling something like, "Brush your teeth—and don't you dare brush one tooth at a time like you did last night."

I'll repeat the proverb to friends when they ask how my kids are. "Oh, you know, driving me mad this week, but hey, it takes a village, right?" We laugh and agree that yes, it does. We'll make plans to "get together soon, for lunch," even though we both know it won't happen for at least three months, because Ally/Adam/Henry/Carly has basketball/piano/Minecraft coding classes/home-work during every free minute we have. That leaves us with precious time sitting alone on a stadium bench or in the car while they practice, relishing the 48 minutes of quiet time, simultaneously hat-ing the fact that we have to wait one more hour to get home. Home, where we can put on pants that make breathing easier, and indulge in a heavenly bath followed by chocolate. But only eaten while in the closet and quietly, because the last time you ate candy in front of the kids, they reminded you that you had not finished your dinner and OH MY GOD THAT IS NOT FAIR!

All this leaves me sitting here wanting to scream, "Where the FUCK is my village?" I want one and I can see it. I actually have it all worked out. We'll all live close to one another in one big, happy neigh-borhood. There will be a communal park where we send our kids directly after school—no playing games or TV until they have had 2.67 hours of outside time. While the kids are playing, the women will congregate at someone's house, whoever's is the cleanest on that particular day. Said house will be required to have good wine and yummy lemonade for those who don't indulge. (I don't know anyone in my neighborhood who doesn't indulge, but it sounds politically correct to have an alternative.) And they must have good chocolate and finger foods. I flipping love finger foods.

We'll gather, and you know what? We'll have the best time ever! These women will be supportive, not spiteful or jealous. We'll lift each other up: "Oh no, Shelley, those pants look amazing on you." We'll say it and mean it. Because hey, if Shelley feels hot in her new pants, I say OWN IT! We'll tell each other, "You look so pretty today," because we love one another and sometimes we look beyond the messy hair, gross yoga pants, and slight smell, and see the beauty inside. And that beauty is oh so pretty! There will be no gossip, because we're all too tired and who needs the extra drain? It will be all about girl power (sans Spice Girls), and we'll just enjoy having someone there who we know has our backs.

If it's been a particularly rough day for Clara, I'll yell, "Send your tyrants over here for a bit," and I'll make a gourmet meal of mac 'n' cheese, hot dogs (uncured and organic of course—wink, wink), and sliced apples. I'll deal with the loudness, the crazy times that come with having a house full of four kids, and I'll feel good. You know why? Because I'll know I'm saving the life of another mother, one who has hit her limit that day and needs this time to unwind. And I'll feel elated knowing that when I hit my bottom limit, Clara will be there for me.

We'll also all have keys to each other's houses. I might come home to find Jocelyn in my closet, because she needed a timeout and it'll be okay. Or Jocelyn might come home to find me at her kitchen table with freshly baked cookies, because I need to stuff my face full of chocolate and butter as I cry about how my sons were once again having a war to see who could fart the loudest, but this time they were taping it with their iPods, because this was going to go on YouTube and make them FAMOUS!

I want my village. I believe in the power of women supporting women. I believe in the need for timeouts. I believe in girl power. I *want* AND *need* this tribe. But until I can find a block of houses for sale and the money to move everyone there, I'll console myself with phone calls to the women who understand—those in the trenches who sometimes find themselves hiding in closets.

But hear me: I have a dream, and I believe it could save the sanity of many women I know. The village is out there. It's calling. And right now, so are my boys because "Moooom, he sat on my head and farted, and now I have his poop air in my hair."

My village.

While visiting my parents, I drank coffee with lunch, napped, had dinner at four, then talked with strangers about my bowels.
Basically, I'm 80.

Chapter 20

Parenting the Parent

I'm at that awkward stage in life where I'm parenting my kids, but often parenting my parents as well—especially when it comes to the confusing and crazy world of electronics and media.

My mom is the worst. She's the lady support specialists dread because it goes something like this:

Tech Support: Ma'am, did you turn on your computer?

Mom: Of course I turned on my computer! I'm not an idiot. That's why I'm calling. It won't start.

Tech Support: Okay, ma'am, exactly what happens when you push the power button?

Mom: Nothing! That's why I'm calling.

Tech Support: Okay, can you power off the computer, wait one minute, and then try again?

Mom: Oh Jesus, okay. Hitting the power button and waiting.

. . .

Mom: Oh! Well, shutting it down seemed to turn it on! It's on now. How the hell did that happen?

Tech Support: I think you turned it off before and just turned it on.

Mom: Oh. Thank you. Good-bye.

My mom has decided now that she's 70, it's time to say "fuck what people think" and embrace the freedom that comes with being 70 and not caring. She's also embracing wearing what she wants and saying what she pleases, and other than declining the freedom to pass gas in public if she sneezes too hard, she's living it up.

This recently included a trip to the local pot shop down the street (we're in a state where it's legal, folks) to try out some of the edibles she's been hearing about. I drove her there and helped her with her oxygen tank into the store. Her COPD requires 24/7 oxygen, and her rheumatoid arthritis makes getting around difficult. We perused the shelves of edibles and asked a few questions, then she happily picked out her lemon drop candies, paid, and left the store with a huge grin.

Two days later, I received this voicemail:

"It's mom. (giggle, snort) Guess what I'm doing?

Ahahahaha. No guess. You won't guess (giggle). Call me back. But guess what I'm doing!"

I guessed.

I called her back and we had a lovely conversation about the lemon drops (they're tasty!) and how her legs and feet were gone. No, not gone, just light. She laughed a lot and said she was hungry and hung up. Over the next several weeks, I noticed things were different.

Here's a usual conversation with my mom when she's trying to get to her email on her iPad.

Mom: Heather, my email is gone again.

Me: No, it's there, you just moved it to the other screen. Swipe left.

Mom: Goddam fucking computer. I hate this piece of shit.

Me: Mom, it's your iPad and you love it. You're just frustrated.

Mom: No, I'm not! I hate it. (To my dad) John, where did my email go? John, goddamit! I did swipe left! Wait, with my right or left hand? Oh, never mind. I did this . . . oh, wait, that was right? Lemme, okay, there. I swiped. There it is!

Me: See, it's still here.

Mom: Oh, don't be so smug.

Me: Sigh.

Here's a conversation with my mom when she's stoned:

Mom: Hi, it's Mom. My iPad ate my email. (giggle). I'd like to eat, I'm hungry. John, can I have some chips?

Me: Mom, swipe left on your iPad. You moved your email icon again.

Mom: I did swipe left. Wait, you mean swipe to the left or with my left hand?

Me: You can swipe with either hand but move your hand to the left.

Mom: Oh, okay. HEY! There's my email! My chips are here, I have to go. Oh wait, guess what I just did?? You won't guess, but try to guess.

I guessed.

When my mom isn't stoned, I often receive texts like this:

Plz cAlLme. I 4got 2 asku a? CALL ME NOW! Asp

On this one I called.

Mom: "Godammit, you never answer your phone! I called your cell, your home, and texted. Obviously you don't care if I'm dead, so I don't need to talk to you."

Me: Mom, if you were dead, you wouldn't have been able to call and text me. What did you need?

Mom: What? Oh Jesus, it's been so long since I called, I don't remember what I needed. Good-bye.

When my mom is stoned, I get texts like this:

CALL ME PLZ I NEED YOU TO CALL ME NOW WHEN YOU CAN TO TALK TO ME BUT PLEZ CALL

For some reason, being stoned activates the caps lock on her phone. So I call.

Me: Hey, Mom, you called?

Mom: What? I did? What did I want?

Me: I don't know, that's why I'm calling back. To see what you needed.

Mom: Oh. (giggle) I don't remember. I feel good. Oh hey, guess what I did? Go on and guess.

I guessed.

When mom's not stoned, here's dinner conversation:

Mom: Your dad's an ass.

Me: What happened?

Mom: I sent him to the store for Depends and he bought the generic version. He's so fucking cheap. And, they don't fit right and leak.

When mom's stoned:

Mom: Your dad's an ass.

Me: Why?

Mom: What?

Me: Why is Dad an ass?

Mom: You watch your mouth, young lady! Your dad just went out and bought me Taco Bell, which is a pretty not assy thing to do. (giggle). I like cheese. Oh, guess what I did?

Now in reading this, it might seem like my non-stoned mom is just angry, and my stoned mom is nice and funny. Who wouldn't like nice and funny better than angry? But that's not the real story. The real story is, when she's stoned, she's not in pain anymore. She lives with the pain of never being able to take a full breath in and having her joints feel like they're on fire. Every day. She lives with having to cart around her oxygen tank everywhere, which makes even a trip to the store seem cumbersome. There are some days she can't open her hands or lift her arm.

So if having a lemon drop every now and then takes away the pain, both mental and physical, I'm all for it. There is nothing I want more than for her to be happy and pain-free. Plus, when she's stoned, I get to play the fun guessing game. I'm getting pretty good at it.

I sneezed this morning and didn't
pee my pants.
Seriously, there should be an
award for this shit.

Chapter 21

40 Makes Me Wet

I've always heard how life-changing and magical it would be to turn 40. I was led to believe I'd feel more settled, more self-assured, more comfortable in my own body, and less worried about what other people think. Personally, I can't say it was a groundbreaking year of self-inquiry and insight, or even a freeing year of finally feeling comfortable in my skin as other women claim. I'm still wrestling with the desire for the elusive flat stomach and less defined laugh lines. I still worry about making a good impression with the other moms at school, and I still want to have great hair days.

What I do know about 40 is that I cry a lot and I pee myself more. Water, water everywhere.

The peeing used to only happen when I'd jump high with my youngest at the trampoline house. I got to where I'd put a pad on to help keep the wet stain from being noticed (thank you, kind mom, for loaning me your sweatshirt to walk to my car that first visit. You're my hero). These days I pee myself regularly.

What gets my panties wet (and not in that way):

- Jumping. Thank you, 10 lb. babies.
- Sneezing, coughing, and even sometimes hiccupping. I need panties with a permanent leak-guard system—you know, something to help save the environment from landfills burdened with Depends. I think I might be onto something here...
- Working out. Oh, the joy that has come from feeling great about the fact that I'm working out, only to have it shattered by realizing my cute workout pants are now darkened with my lady-bit drips. And because I am me, they're inside out.
- Laughing. Which usually makes me laugh more (from mortification), which then leads to hiccupping. It's a clusterfuck.
- Crying. Yes, when I'm sobbing too hard, my girl cave gets jealous and wants to cry too.

This last one leads me into the other thing that

I've discovered since being 40: I cry at everything. I've always been the woman who cries during the sad scenes in movies or when the girl and guy finally get together at the end of the book. Now I seem to cry at the most inane things.

Reasons I've cried just this week:

- I peed myself. Okay, as I just told you, this has become a regular thing, and given that crying also makes me pee, sometimes I feel like I should just spend my days on the toilet.
- Adele sang "Hello" on the *TODAY Show* and it was beautiful.
- I ran out of wine. I was sobbing and my husband went and bought me a bottle. That made me cry too.
- I punched myself in the cheek trying to get the fitted sheet on the bed.
- I happened to catch a glimpse of myself yawning in the mirror. Have you ever looked at yourself yawning?
- I found a forgotten tub of Chunky Monkey in the freezer when I was looking for chicken. So happy!
- I ate the whole tub of Chunky Monkey.

- My son didn't want to spend time with me.
- My son wouldn't leave me alone and followed me everywhere, even to pee, which yeah, I know could happen anywhere, but this was actually a full pee stop in the bathroom.

I could go on, but I'm starting to get embarrassed.

I had high hopes for 40. Now I have high hopes for 42. I'm clinging to the idea that at some point, I'll feel so confident in myself (because, life experience, right?) that I won't care if I pee. I'll embrace the warmth and count myself lucky to have my two beautiful (gross) boys. What's a little pee in my panties compared to the joy of looking for missing socks or arguing with my teen about why he should use soap in the shower, not just water? I'm hoping to finally feel comfortable in the body I have, not the body I want. I hope to hold my head high at the school carnival, as the other PTA moms cluster and talk shop, even if I am the mom whose son is running around screaming, "I like pink fluffy unicorns who dance and fart rainbows!"

What? Your sons **don't** like unicorns?

In the end I have hope, and that's enough to

get me up each morning and think, "Maybe today is the day I stay dry." Thank you, 40, for showing me what true priorities are.

My thighs clap when I run.
I'm choosing to think of it as my
private cheering squad, clapping with
each step I take.
Perspective.

Chapter 22

Caution: Low-Hanging Boobs

Okay, so I'm past 40 now and still waiting for this whole *amazing* thing that was supposed to happen to me—feeling comfortable in my skin, not caring what people think when I go out with my yoga pants on inside out, finally embracing my body, scars and all. I'm supposed to turn my attention toward growing old gracefully and gratefully, let go of the idea of female perfection as attainable. I read about women over 40 having this shift happen for them, and every fiber of my being wants to scream, "Yes, yes, yes! I love me just as I am, and I'm going to throw out these too-small clothes, buy a new wardrobe, and celebrate with a box of my favorite chocolates—and wine." But if I sit back and ask myself if this is true, I must admit, it's *not*.

Below are some reasons I haven't fully (and lovingly) embraced aging.

- My breasts now rest comfortably on my

stomach unless I'm lying down. Then they're under my armpits.

- I've gained 10 lbs.—seemingly from eating apples. I know it's not the wine because there was an article going around saying wine is equivalent to gym time, so it's a proven scientific fact that it's good for me. Screw apples.

- I'm wet. All. The. Time. Whether it's from crying over some ridiculous thing (like my boobs being on my stomach), or the fact that I wet myself with every sneeze or cough.

- I forget stuff. Important stuff like, you know, *words*. Trying to tell my husband that the neighborhood potholes were "posing a … you know, that bad thing … a bad thing for people?" The word was "danger."

- The arm waddle. You know that skin under your arms that keeps waving, long after you've stopped? That.

- I can't party anymore. I discovered the miracle of wine late in life, but I can't seem to have more than seven small glasses before I pass out on the couch, drooling. It sucks because, gym time, remember??

- My hormones have taken over, and I often have no clue who I am anymore. Coupled with periods that often make my bathroom look like a crime scene, this ensures I'm never wanting for drama in my life.

I'm sure there's more, but guess what? I can't remember it! I know I should embrace this and be joyful that everyone I love is healthy. I have an amazing life and am blessed and trust me, I am and I do. But, when I go into my closet looking for the miracle outfit that makes me look put together and allows me to breathe, I get defeated. I'll cheer myself up with the promise of chocolate or a nice bottle of wine and . . . you see the problem.

I know I'm not alone; I know my village of women is out there, reading this and whispering, "Yes, me too, yes!" I am writing this to you, my friends, to let you know that you are not alone. That I, too, can tie my boobs in a knot and can't recall that hot actor's name, you know, the one in that movie? I also jiggle, which causes me to pee and cry at random times, in my closet with my wine. I hide in the pantry and eat the good chocolate and tell myself my diet starts tomorrow. I, too, will be asleep at eight p.m., drooling, and will wake at two a.m. to pee and then again at five because my bladder hates me.

We're not alone. We're survivors, happily wetting ourselves, waving as we pass, arm flab flapping, as we inch toward menopause.

MENOPAUSE??!!

I give up.

There's a reason the first three letters in "diet" are die.

Chapter 22

The Secret to Dieting

With the whole getting older thing, I've gained weight. So, I started doing what I do best—which is doing a ton of research on what is the *best* possible way to have healthy skin/hair/nails/sleep/sex-drive/skinny-waist/strong bones. I want to wake in the morning energized, refreshed, and have energy to spare by the end of the day. I want my skin to glow and I want to ROCK my jeans!

The information is out there, but it can be daunting to read through everything, look up the science behind the claims, and then to try and find recipes for foods you actually want to eat. (Have you tried tempeh? It's sadness in a cube!) Since I've spent so much time reading, I figured I would make your life easier and summarize everything for you.

Breakfast:

Smoothies! Oh, the varieties available are astounding. Like this one:

1 c. chopped red cabbage

1/2 red bell pepper

1 Roma tomato

5 medium strawberries

1/2 c. raspberries

8 oz. cold water

1 ice cube [optional]—(just one, because too much ice is . . . cold)

If you want to know what despair tastes like, make that.

I decided to start with almond milk, kale, protein powder, banana, and blueberries—sweet and filling. Then I read that's too much fruit sugar first thing in the morning, so I cut out the fruit.

Oh, and protein powders with sweeteners are bad (natural or artificial, unless it's from Stevia, which is okay because it's plant based. Oh wait, that's not okay because it still confuses your pancreas), and the powders without sweeteners taste like ass, so I cut that out.

A recent study showed almond milk is hardly

"almond" at all and mostly fillers, so I just used water.

So, water and kale smoothie. Or eggs. Lots and lots of eggs.

Lunch:

Wraps—these are so wonderfully versatile! I opted not to get the paleo wraps, which consisted of coconut meat, coconut water, and coconut oil. I just couldn't. Instead I opted for whole grain, high protein tortilla wraps filled with turkey lunchmeat, spinach, hummus, and tomato.

Then I researched the alkaline diet that my massage therapist recommended, which says grains are bad, and I read that overall, lunchmeat is bad, even the organic kind. So, I cut out the wrap and the turkey, which was okay since the tortilla was dry, hard, and tasted like wood.

Then a friend told me hummus is hard for your body to digest—it's the beans—and causes excess gas and bloating, so that was out.

So, spinach and tomato, on . . . a plate.

Dinner:

I really thought I had this one figured out. I

would do some lean protein or fish, quinoa, and a salad.

Meat needs to be from cows that were grass fed, lived outdoors, suckled until they felt ready to ween, cuddled at least 30 minutes daily, and lived within a 50-mile radius of my house (something to do with local allergens or some voodoo). I couldn't find that meat at my local grocery store, so meat was out. Fish needs to be wild caught and sustainable, and even then, it probably has microbeads in it, so I stayed away from fish.

Okay, I could still do some yummy quinoa and salad.

But then I remembered grains are bad (by now, I'm so effing hungry I can't recall why), and on some diets, you can't eat grains and veggies at the same time because it messes up the digestive process and enzymes. Fuck.

I'm left with salad.

Dessert:

There is no dessert! And don't try and sell me on the frozen banana-only ice cream or the gluten-free, sugar-free, grain-free, taste-free cakes either. I can tell the difference. I'm on to you!

You can have an apple. Doesn't that sound

yummy and all comfort food-like? You simply bake it for a bit, with a dash of cinnamon, so it tastes just like NO APPLE PIE EVER!

Key takeaways:

You can eat spinach, kale, and tomato. And water.

OR . . .

You can do what I did and go to See's candy, get a box of chocolates to pair with your delicious wine or cocktail of choice, and smile again.

But only the small box because, hello—DIET!

Bucket list item #5 DONE!
Attended a yoga class last night.
Only fell asleep once and didn't pass
gas the entire time.
It's all about goals.

Chapter 23

Lessons Learned from My Solo Vacation

Last year, I took my first ever solo vacation. Just me, myself, and I, and we all had a wonderful time. I went to Red Mountain Resort in Utah, which might now be at the top of my Favorite Places Ever list, along with my bed and the candy store. It's all about health, wellness, knowledge, and being mindful.

I met some super sweet women, ate delicious food, slept, and worked out. It was amazing. Not only did I have a wonderful time, I learned a *lot*—about my body (including my butt), my mind, food, sleep, people, and my limits.

Below are some of the top takeaways from my trip. Hopefully, they'll help you, whether in your daily life or on a solo vacation.

Top Four Things I Learned on My Solo Vacation:

1.   *Mindful eating is easy.*

Mindful eating is all about no longer mindlessly shoveling food into your mouth and searching your plate for the next bite while you're still chewing. It's thinking about the food in your mouth, while you eat. It's about slowing down and appreciating your food, exploring the tastes and textures, and *being in the now* while you eat. Stop thinking about your to-do list or the fact that you need to shave your legs (while I can mindfully eat, I can't mindfully write when I need to shave my legs). One morning, I mindfully ate my weight in bacon. I thought about the bacon, I loved the bacon, and I enjoyed every moment. I *can* learn!

2.   *Understand the company you keep.*

Because so many of us were traveling solo, they had a communal dining table each night to encourage meeting others. My first dinner there, I raved about the bread, ordered a glass of wine, and requested two desserts (they're really small desserts, people). As I was eating my (first) dessert, people started talking about why they were at the resort, and I found out that *everyone* at the table was on a weight loss retreat. I'm sure they sincerely appreciated my gushing about the carb-loaded bread, how much I was enjoying my wine, and ordering a second dessert. Know your company.

3. *When you eat healthy, a lot of things happen.*

Let's just say, when you eat a ton of veggies, fruit, fish, and lean meat, coupled with lots of water, fresh air, sunshine, and working out, stuff in you begins to move. And eventually it moves right out of you. Like a shit ton of stuff. Enough said. Just be prepared and enjoy the lightness of being.

4. *People can lose control on vacation.*

It happened a lot in the workout classes, as well as in the meditation, yoga, and relaxation classes. People simply lost control. One woman was bending to jump up from the Bosa ball and she lost control . . . of her butt. I did a pretty good job of not losing control of my laughter as I tried to continue the workout. (I was also now very aware of my own butt.) It also happened in the relaxation classes, but this time it was me. I fell asleep. I think I kept my butt in check, but who knows? I was asleep and yes, I snored.

Those are only a few of the funnier things I learned on my vacation. I did, however, have some poignant "a-ha" moments too. Like when I realized I enjoyed being alone. Until I didn't. Then I needed someone to talk to, even if it was just the young table busser, who didn't really know what to make of my nonstop questions about his life goals. When I saw he was chewing gum, I tried to make a little joke about how he should take the time to think about the gum. Where did it come from, and how was it making him feel? I think I scared the poor boy. My water glass stayed empty the rest of my meal. I also learned that two massages in one week is totally doable, *but,* in a place like this, you must be very aware of falling asleep. And your butt.

Getting away from reality for a week, alone, was a great motivator to come back to life refreshed, energized, and ready to put into action all the plans I laid out while there.

After being back for two weeks, I managed to buy the book I wanted to read about mindfulness.

I have yet to start it, but at least I bought it so

don't hate. And I stocked the wine fridge, opting to ease back into this whole real-life thing.

It was hard.

Some days I feel like I should have a tag that says, "Some assembly required."

Chapter 24

9 Things I Wish Someone Had Told Me About Getting a Hysterectomy

As I write this chapter, I am nine days past having a partial hysterectomy. They left my ovaries but took my cervix, uterus, and fallopian tubes. It feels like they yanked out all my internal organs, played soccer with them, put them back, then filled me with a bunch of air and sealed it tightly inside me with some glue.

I've spent too much time focusing on my lady bits. Insane periods, crime scene bathrooms, cramps and backaches that left me immobile. My periods were always long—seven days—but now they were two weeks, sometimes more. I was on birth control, but I would start a period in the middle of a pack of pills. I was tired. Worn out. I was sick of taking pills, sick of surprise periods, sick of the pain, and I needed it to stop.

My OB suggested I consider a hysterectomy, unless I wanted more children. Once I recovered from the fit of laughing (the three boys in my house is plenty), I agreed it was time.

I had done research on laparoscopic hysterectomy, and everything I read was uplifting. Less downtime, pain, and scarring than the regular kind. I bought a book on how to prepare for surgery and how I could help my healing. I read feedback forums from women who'd had the procedure. Mainly they gushed about living in Period-Free Blissland.

Period-free—sign me up!

Leading up to the surgery I made sure that I ate healthy, worked out, and got rest. I meditated, repeating positive affirmations in my head, like, "I will have a safe and successful surgery and I will heal easily." I drank bone broth and green smoothies, took probiotics (because, HEALTH), and drank Kombucha (because, INSANE). I tried to be the epitome of Zen, but there was a huge part of me that was scared.

Despite my preparation, I truly was not prepared for what was to come. My doctor had told me that if everything went well during the surgery, and if I was able to walk and urinate without issue afterward, I could go home that day. He said some women do. He also said some women feel great a few days later. Some women don't even need pain pills.

I assumed I was going to be one of those women. Then reality bitch slapped me and put me in my place.

Surgery went great—I walked, I peed, *and* I kept my tired ass in that hospital bed the rest of the day and overnight.

In case you're not "some women," here are a few things you might want to prepare for, so that you don't feel bitch slapped like I did.

1. You might wake from surgery shaking like you've just run a 300k. Now, I've never even run a 5k, but if I ran a 300k, I'd probably shake like that.

2. You'll be in twilight and hear them say, "Let's give her some Demerol for the shaking." Then a blissful calm will envelop you, at which point you'll wake, look at the nurse, and say, "You're so pretty. Have I said how pretty you are? Wow, you're pretty." I think she was flattered but also a little creeped out.

3. You'll soon realize you have so much air inside you that you could single-handedly blow up

enough balloons to rival the house in the movie *Up*. AND IT WON'T COME OUT! This isn't just gas, this is air inside your body cavity. They fill you with air so that your organs will shift, allowing them to see and work inside you. Once they're done, they just seal you up like a big human balloon, and you have to wait for your body to absorb the air. Enter pain meds. They'll inject beautiful, blissland medicine into your IV, and for a while all is right with the world.

4. Peeing will take like 10–15 minutes. Plus, you need to move into approximately eight different positions to get it out. I found having my husband lift my feet off the floor and hold them up was the most helpful. Bless that man.

5. If you're a coffee drinker, drink some caffeine as soon as you can to avoid the withdrawal headache. Mine morphed into a full-blown migraine, which had me begging for them to hurry and get me migraine meds. Ahhh, meds.

6. Everything might hurt. For more than a few days. I felt like something might fall out every time I stood up. (Note: Nothing did.)

7. It might hurt to eat. I developed some crazy stomach cramping when I would eat anything more than broth or a smoothie. It might have been the Tylenol and Advil, so I stopped that pretty quick-

ly. But hey—I lost weight! Four pounds in a week, which is a record for me. Sigh.

8. Let's get real about this—pooping. Oh, Holy Mother of God! This was by far the worst. I couldn't go. I needed to, and it hurt so badly. I'd been taking the stool softeners—no luck. So, my husband went and got a fiber drink. No luck. My husband went and got some suppositories. A little luck. Then my husband went and bought Milk of Magnesia. That, plus some light walking on the treadmill (walk, walk, walk if you can!), brought a little more luck. Then my husband went and got an enema and prune juice. Bingo! Basically, my husband bought the entire section of bowel remedies in three days. Bless that man (again).

9. You might look a little pregnant. I guess I look about four months along. Bloat, inflammation, plus not using your ab muscles (hey, did you know you use your ab muscles for like EVERYTHING???) makes for a small non-baby, baby bump. It'll go away, but have some loose-fitting clothes handy.

10. Finally, have a person! Have someone with you who can help. My husband was my person, and if there was an award for Best Husband, he would win. That man helped me off the couch, made me food, got me water, and rubbed my shoulders when the pain from the gas was searing. He

listened to me cry and rubbed my head. He fed my dog. He helped me shower, drying my legs because I couldn't bend over. He was my hero, and there aren't enough words or gestures in the world to let him know how thankful I am.

I removed parts of me that caused pain, frustration, and inconvenience. I removed parts of me that bore two beautiful boys, the parts that created them, carried them, and put them into my arms. I removed actual parts of me, and my body is working to make me whole again. What a friggen miracle we are!

Nine days out and today I feel human! I still have some slight pain, but I'm on the mend. I looked in the mirror last night, taking in my five small incisions, my bloated belly, my sallow skin, makeup-less face, and messy hair, and I swear to you, ladies, I was amazed at the beauty. It's beautiful what my body is doing. My body has been through something major and traumatic and it's healing. It's working for me, doing awe-inspiring things to get me back to 100% health.

If you're going down this road, my main suggestion is to be kind to yourself. Know that you might be like "some women," or you might be just like you. You'll have your own story and your own recovery, and everything that happens will be just what is supposed to happen to you. Be gentle, relax, sleep, take the pain meds if you need them, and let people help. Let them bring you food, go to the store, or hold your feet up in the hospital so you can eke out a few more drops.

Oh, you do CrossFit?
Today I got stuck in my sports bra,
ran from a bee, and lifted a big box
of wine from my car.
We're even, right?

Chapter 25

My Day of Shame

It began when I ate the bug. The sun was out and I decided to take my dog for a walk before my eye exam. I didn't mean to eat the bug, but in my defense, I didn't see it flying directly toward my mouth. By the time I knew there was a bug, I was smacking my mouth, spitting, and making horrid sounds and faces trying to get the poor bug *out* of my mouth. I really tried but finally just swallowed, smiling at the couple who had witnessed the whole horror show.

My dog had the urge to go, so he began to do the walk where he curls in on himself and turns in circles. I always feel like I've won the lottery if he goes in four circles or less. Today was six, but I was already kind of losing after the whole bug-eating thing. He found the perfect spot and crouched, then I looked down in time to see his back foot rise and plant right down into the poo he'd just made. Joy.

After I had the honor of dragging his paw through the only one-inch circle of grass nearby, then picking up after him, we continued. I was wearing earbuds listening to a book when I felt the urge to . . . fluff (toot, make wind—whatever). Figuring I'm outside so no biggie, I let it go, then suddenly remembered that only I was wearing earbuds. I looked around and was mortified to see a man behind me (I didn't make eye contact) and a man up on the hill to my left. I cleared my throat loudly, coughed a little (you know that move? Make *more* noise to call attention to yourself), and picked up my pace.

I was regretting not bringing lip balm for my chapped lips when a woman walked by and smiled. I smiled back, causing my bottom lip to split painfully. Grabbing my lip, I LOUDLY exclaimed (because, earbuds), "Oh, shit. Ouch!" That was not the friendly impression I was hoping to leave. Same thing when the woman with the big dogs walked by and I shouted, "ARE THEY FRIENDLY?"

Basically, I'm a dumbass.

On to my eye exam.

Disclaimer: I hate eyeballs.

Anyone who knows me knows this. I'm the

person who gets something in her eye and freaks out, because there's no way I'm sticking my finger in there. Anyhow, I was feeling an insane amount of pride, since I was *finally* able—for the first time— to do that test, where they violently squirt air into your eye (shudder). I was probably *too* prideful, because the universe came back to kick my butt.

In the eye doctor's tiny office, I did all the normal tests. Then I confessed I was worried I was getting that old person thing, where they get that yellow goopy stuff over their eyeballs. Because in the morning when I look in the mirror, I swear I have goopy stuff on my left eye. She took a look, and I just knew she was going to tell me I had it and then I'd have to ask for new eyeballs.

"Nope, you don't have that, but I'll tell you what you do have," she said and started talking. And talking. But she wasn't telling me what I had.

I thought, "WHAT IS IT? FOR THE LOVE OF GOD, TELL ME!"

She must have heard me telepathically, because at that point she said, "You have dry eyes and need drops."

Then it happened.

I began sweating. I felt like I was going to crap my pants. The room spun and I said I didn't feel well. She told me to close my eyes and relax. That made it worse, and I announced I was going to pass out. I asked if I could lie on the floor and BAM! Next thing I knew, I was on the floor. When I came to, my feet were up on the exam chair and I was a sweaty mess. I peeled off my sweater; I worried I might soil myself. After the doc brought me some water, I was finally able to sit up.

She received the BEST DOCTOR EVER award because she told me it had happened before. Lots of people get dizzy and some pass out. I don't know if that's true, but it did help make me feel better.

I'll stay out of the real world for a bit, since obviously, I don't know how to behave in public anymore. I should be thankful that I didn't walk in wearing my tiara and that I didn't *actually* soil myself on the exam room floor.

I choose to be grateful for the little things.

Me getting ready to go out on a Friday: So excited to get to hang with everyone!
Me after one hour of hanging: People suck and I miss my bed.

Chapter 26

I Suck at This Whole "Being Social" Thing

I'm a social gal. I like people. I enjoy parties, meeting new people, and finger food. I adore finger food. But I have anxiety when I'm going to a party where I'll be socializing with folks I don't know well. Which exactly describes the neighborhood party we'd been invited to. I'd met most of the neighbors but it was usually a quick intro, where I couldn't tell you their names five minutes later.

There would be a white elephant gift exchange (Oh God, do I bring a real gift or try to go for the cool/silly/funny/alcoholic gift?) All the neighbors had RSVP'd and my husband could only come for about 30 minutes, because he agreed I should socialize while he watched our boys. They could be left alone for 30 minutes, but anything more would ensure someone would get hurt, break something, or get a bad tummy ache because they'd found

Mommy's secret candy stash.

I put on a new dress because Mommy's secret candy stash had been calling, and Mommy could no longer fit into anything in the closet. I felt like I looked pretty put together for a half insane mom of three boys.

We walked in and the anxiety hit me hard when I saw there were way more people there than lived in the 'hood, so I knew friends, family, and probably coworkers were there too. Their house looked like something out of a *Pretty Homes You'll Never Be Able to Recreate* magazine, and the entire kitchen was made into a wonderland of holiday cheer.

"There's a mixologist downstairs if you'd like to grab a drink," the host said, "and we have a fun game to get people talking. Ask people you don't know the questions on this paper, write them down, and put it in the box. We'll draw a name for a fun prize!"

I love prizes! After my husband and I visited the mixologist, I turned around with my drink and ran into . . . my EX Boss! Yep, he'd moved into the neighborhood recently. Joy. I worked for him years ago while going through my divorce, and he'd fired me. Anyway, I saw him and downed my drink, avoiding him as long as I could. Then I ordered another drink. And that's when things started to go south.

This is why I'll never be invited to another neighborhood party:

- A neighbor asked me one of the game questions—what my favorite holiday tradition was—and I replied, "My husband likes to get drunk and dress up like Santa, then try to fit down the chimney. We have fun seeing if he'll fit." I giggled as he looked at me blankly and left.

- I noticed my husband talking to a very busty, tightly dressed, high-heeled, big-haired woman. She was laughing and touching his arm when he saw me and gave me the "Help!" eye signal. I walked up, he introduced me, and she merely smiled . . . and walked away! I thought I was whispering when I said, "How bitchy," but since she turned around, as did the couple next to me, I realized I needed to work on my whispering. I have three boys, for goodness' sake. I never whisper and am out of practice!

- I was enjoying piling my plate with amazing finger food when my son called asking when I would be home because he had a tummy ache. My son always has tummy aches so I wasn't concerned. I was getting frustrated with his whining when I exclaimed, "You can poop alone. You don't need me! . . . No, it's weird to have people hang out with you while you poop!" *Again, working on my inside voice.* I apologized to the people at the finger food table for not taking my call outside.

- My husband asked if I was okay, I assured him I was, and he left. I was doing better thanks to my drinks, but I probably should have eaten sooner. The next woman I met was pregnant. I figured this was safe ground, so I asked her when she was due. "I'm not pregnant," she said. "Oh . . . neither am I!" I exclaimed. Drink #3.

- The hosts had the most amazing wall hanging downstairs: a giant Scrabble board. I love Scrabble and proceeded to try and spell something. Sheila came down and said, "Oh, that's just for decoration. That's way too delicate to actually play with." I had a 42-point word too!

- I eventually ran into my ex-boss again and decided to be mature. I said hi and asked where his wife was. "She left me. We're getting a divorce." Before I was even aware I had spoken, I heard myself say, "OMG, I SO called that!" I apologized, but really, I did call it and was feeling kind of bitchy myself.

- I was chatting with a woman who has two daughters and said, "It must be awesome having girls. You get the fun letter Ps: pink, princesses, and ponies. The three Ps I get are piss, penises, and punching." She excused herself and I didn't see her the rest of the evening.

It's embarrassing putting this down on paper so I'll stop. No need to detail my neighbor's reaction when, after talking about her two "adorable, sweet, and amazingly smart" young boys, I told her how mine used to be that way and now spend their evenings trying to outfart one another. Oh! And how they recently put a full-sized doughnut in the toilet for target practice, since I used to put Cheerios in there when they were potty training. Cheerios, of course, are too small now.

I tell myself we're not "that" family, that lots of people have an extra two or three drinks when nervous. Lots of moms get fed up with farts and yell they'll tape their sons' buttholes shut if they don't stop farting, and their sons think that sounds like great fun and actually do it.

We're normal . . . right? Invite us over to your

next party and find out. We're sure to bring lots of
conversation starters!

"At least he was polite."
Me, after my son says to Santa,
"I'm sorry I farted on your leg."
Perspective, folks.

Chapter 27

What Mommy Wants for Christmas

When my boys were twelve, eleven, and seven, I wasn't sure what to expect for the holidays. In truth, twelve- and eleven-year-old boys are too old to be holding onto the whole "Santa is real" thing, but alas, they were holding on so tight that if Santa was real, his fat little belly would explode. I was keeping up with the charade but let's be honest, I was finding it hard not to just blurt out, "Oh seriously, dude, Santa is not coming down our chimney since for one, we don't even HAVE a chimney, and two, he will NOT bring you a new iPad, because HE'S NOT REAL!"

It was still cool for Gavin to believe, though. I really wanted him to have a few more years of holiday magic. But the two older ones were a different story. Once Aidan asked when I thought he might be able to start masturbating, I kind of figured

Santa was out the window. Joke was on me! I was actually looking forward to the day I could get him in on the fun. He could oversee the creepy-ass Elf on the Shelf, and he could help put out the Santa gifts at one a.m., when his brother finally conked out from having gotten up every eight minutes for the past four hours to check and see if Santa had come. Then I'd wake Aidan at five a.m. and make him come downstairs and open his gifts—and *no* nap that day. He would have all the fun while I'd relax in the bath with a good book and some cookies we baked for Santa. But, I digress.

Since I still had to do the whole Santa thing for the boys that year, I figured I would just add my own gift list to the pile, in hopes that someone might review it and be so kind as to indulge *me* this year.

What Mommy Wants:

1. I'd like for Aidan to give me the silent treatment for one day. No really, punish me—PLEASE.

2. I'd like to take a bath without someone coming in to:

    • Tell on his brother for trying to fill his new whoopee cushion with actual farts

- "See if I'm okay," then laugh because I have bubbles on my boobs, then call me "Bubble Boobs" the rest of the night
- Hang out. Seriously, it's just weird.
- Ask what time it is. Guys, there are 15 clocks in the house, none of which are in MY BATHROOM!

3. A foot rub. And before anyone complains they just gave me one, a foot rub that's longer than the 2.34 seconds of bliss of foot rubs past.

4. My panty liners to stay in the box. I know they ended up making the most awesome "butter-fly art" for your girlfriend down the street, but let's keep our crafts sanitary-napkin-free, okay? Plus, her mom thought it was pretty weird, so now we have that going for us.

5. Chocolate. Lots and lots of chocolate.

6. Someone to play Scrabble with me. Just one game and I promise to forget I majored in English.

7. An afternoon of baking while holiday music plays and I sip Bailey's coffee. Then someone to come and clean it all up.

8. For the Elf on the Shelf to have a heart attack and die. I'll even go so far as to have a proper funeral.

9. If you can't manage even one of these, just tell me I'm pretty!

Honestly, I didn't think I was asking for much, given everything I do for everyone else (HELLO, house full of testosterone—toilets, walls, doors, and ceilings don't clean themselves of the pee!), and the fact that I do (most) of it without complaint. I think anyone would agree a little complaining is fair when your kid comes out of the bathroom, holding his underwear, and says, "I ran out of toilet paper so I used these. I was trying to be nice and let you enjoy your book, so I didn't call for toilet paper. Here."

So, this is the list I gave my boys and husband.

I got the chocolate. I'd already taken care of the Bailey's.

You might be a mom if . . . You've ever been woken at two a.m. to hear, "My blanket fell on the floor. Help me."

Chapter 28

I'm Not Ready

My boys just celebrated their birthdays. As you already know, they were both born in April, five years apart. It not only makes for a very hectic April, but the birthdays are getting harder. They're growing older and pulling away, friends are more important than family, voices are deepening, smells are stronger, and the blackheads are insane. (My son refuses to let me squeeze them. Too gross?)

And FORTHELOVEOFGODCANITSTOP because I'm not ready!

Don't get me wrong, I'm poised to tackle the tween and teen years coming. The moodiness, the eye rolls, the "oh my GOD you are so dumb" mutterings, and the smell (always the smell). I'm not saying it'll be easy, but I'm as prepared as I can be. I'm not, however, ready to say good-bye.

There have been so many good-byes recently. Good-bye to the thumb-sucking and hair-twirling that signaled Aidan's tiredness. Good-bye to the "long blinks" that Gavin used to take almost every time we got into a car. Good-bye to lazy mornings in bed cuddling, while sleep still held on and they smelled like joy. Good-bye to trips to the park, which would light up both their faces like Disneyland, and the laughter that would come from the swings, the slide, and the life they were experiencing. Good-bye to curling up on the couch and watching some horrible kids' cartoon or movie—over, and over, and over again. Good-bye to singing them to sleep at night, us curled into one.

Good-bye to my babies.

Being a mother is the hardest thing I have ever done, and these days I don't always enjoy it. There are days I want to run away when the fights are too loud, homework is missing, dinner is being scoffed at, and I am so tired I can hardly stand. I want to say my own good-bye and drive away. I complain a lot, about my fear for their futures, my frustrations at their current actions, and my insecurities about how I'm handling the whole mother thing. Even though all of this is true, even though I feel out of control and overwhelmed more days than not, even though this is hard, I still don't want to say good-bye just yet. I'm not ready.

Every single thing I read, hear from someone

with grown kids, or see in sappy movies says to me, "Cherish this time. It goes by so fast." And still I've rolled my eyes and wanted to scream, "It's not fast enough!"

Then I find myself realizing my babies are going to be a year older soon, and holy shit, it really does go by fast. I'm looking at them both and wanting to grab Gavin's still slightly chubby cheeks and Aidan's skinny, gangly arms and hold on for dear life.

"Stop!" I want to yell. "Stop growing. Stop leaving me!"

I know it's not about me; I know this is the way of things. I know tomorrow I will wake and they both will be fighting and tattling, and I will once again be overwhelmed. I want to rewind so I can right my wrongs, hug instead of yell, laugh at the spilled milk (and juice, and ice cream, and and and). But that's not how life works. And while I would love to say I will take this feeling into the weekend, into next week, and into this whole year and be the perfect mother, I won't. I will fail. Sometimes daily, other times maybe only once a week, but I will fail.

So, I have right now, this minute to imprint this feeling of having to let go while still frantically holding on. The feelings of regret, sadness, love, and joy are all wrapped around one another so tightly, I couldn't separate them if I tried.

On the eve of you both becoming one year older, one year further away from being my babies, I want you to know this: You're loved. Everything I've done in this world since the moment you both came into it has been done with you in mind. There will never again be a day in my life when I don't think of you, when I don't worry about you, or when I don't want to be able to deliver you all the joy in the world to you on a platter.

There will never be a day when I'm ready to give all that up.

Just bit down on a Lego in my brownie.

Reason #437 not to bake with kids.

Chapter 29

Our Kitchen

A Love Letter to My Boys

It's where we began. Our kitchen. It was the hub of our family—where we cooked, ate, laughed, played with the pots and pans, looked out the window while doing dishes, and imagined. We remembered and lost ourselves in thought.

It's where you grew up.

It's where you both taught me that no toy could compare to the fun and excitement of banging on pots with a wooden spoon, or using silicone baking cups with a bowl full of watery bubbles to create your own brand of art. I remember the chubby hands, covered in soapy fun, touching my cheek. I remember the smile, baby teeth still perfect, cheeks still holding onto toddler plumpness. I remember the way your hair curled, the way you would twirl it with your fingers and suck your thumb, coated in soap and all. I remember you, Aidan, showing your baby brother how to make bubble art, how you both laughed so hard it hurt to take a breath because there was almost no room with all the joy you were inhaling.

I remember the time the two of you baked banana bread together—standing on chairs, one reading directions and one holding the spoon. You were both so proud of yourselves. I remember our breakfasts around the table—no TV, no distractions, just us, talking about the day, the dreams you'd each had the night before. That table held your Lego creations, the remnants of your Play-Doh masterpieces. We filled it with our cookies, breads, and fudge each holiday. I wiped baby handprints of mashed sweet potatoes and peas from its top, and then later, toddler fingerprints, and too soon, young boy handprints.

It's where you stood one morning, dish towel draped ceremoniously over your arm, as you welcomed me to my table, where you'd prepared a wonderful breakfast of yogurt with sugar sprinkles, toast with butter on one half, and coffee with so much creamer it was nearly white. You boys had worked so hard to prepare breakfast for me as a surprise that the love I felt for you both took my breath away.

It's where we began each birthday, the table set with a plate full of sprinkled doughnuts, a fruit salad, and each of your gifts, brightly wrapped and full of potential fun. It's where we ate birthday pizzas and tacos and hamburgers, laughing and enjoying the passing of another year. We marked each of your inches on the corner wall in red, amazed to see how quickly the marks were rising.

It's where I have some of my happiest memories, the kitchen.

We've now moved and our kitchen is not the same. With the move came the passing of time, and with time came you each growing apart. The fights are more frequent, the harsh words more cutting. Our new kitchen is bigger and at times, I'm lost. I miss the four close walls where we would get lost too, but in the joys of childhood. I miss your laughter as you both slid around the kitchen floor being worms, or dogs, or whatever mythical creature you'd dreamt up that morning.

I miss our kitchen.

I miss those days of being young. I'm struggling now to figure out this new role I play, no longer having my cheek caressed with soapy hands or seeing the joy on your faces when you make me breakfast. I understand this is how it must be, and I'll be patient until we get through the harder years while you pull away more and more.

I'll wait.

I'll try not to fight it, but I won't always be successful. And when the day comes, when you and your brother are once again in the kitchen as grown men, laughing about your own family's antics, I'll feel at ease again. I'll pull out the pots and pans. I'll pull out the wooden spoon and bowl, and I'll fill it with warm, soapy water. And the joy will engulf me once again as I watch your kids experience the joy of childhood.

In the kitchen.

"When I grow up, my main goal is to be a dad. I'll have seven kids because kids are *FUN!*"

—Aidan, age 11

"*AHAHAHA!*"

—Me, age 39

Chapter 30

I've Been Dismissed

I was not prepared. I'm not sure any mom ever is, no matter how well informed we are, how many studies we read, or how much we think we know about this gig called parenting. The night it happened, I left Aidan's room in shock. "How did this happen so fast?" I thought. "Why did I not see this coming? What now?"

For a few days, Aidan had been asking me to watch a TV show with him that he loves. I finally got Gavin down at a decent time and happily walked into Aidan's room announcing, "I'm here. Let's watch the show." He was so excited to share this with me that he jumped up and turned on his computer. He immediately began giving away the entire plot line, telling me all about the characters I was about to get to know and who was and wasn't still on the show (he'd already watched through to season four). He settled himself next to me and pushed play.

I was pleased to find that I actually liked the show. We used to spend our evenings before bed-time watching old sitcoms from the 90s, which he and I both loved, especially *Friends*. It made me happy to see we'd found another show we could enjoy together, something for just him and me to do—together.

Then she called.

Aidan has an awesome friendship with a girl he has known since kindergarten. They always ended up in the same class together until he moved schools two years ago. Thanks to the genius that is technology, they've kept in contact and spend most of their nights on FaceTime with each other— doing nothing. I'm not sure they even talk; they're simply "with" one another. She is hands-down the sweetest girl I have ever met. She's beautiful, she's always smiling, and she's a good soul.

But when she called that night, my world changed.

"Emily's calling," he said.

"Tell her you're hanging with your favorite gal and you'll call her back," I replied. (See how cool I am with my hip lingo?)

He texted back exactly what I had said (favorite gal and all), and we continued.

She called again. And again. "She says she can

only talk for a few more minutes before she has to go to bed," he said, looking at me sadly.

I knew what he wanted. And I knew he was torn. He'd been begging me to watch the show for ages. But EMILY was calling.

"You want me to step out so you can talk to her?" I asked, half hoping he would say no.

"Okay. We can watch this in the morning or tomorrow night, I promise," he said, hugging me.

I hugged him back and realized I'd been replaced.

I walked out and I ached. I longed for the days when he would twirl my hair and suck his thumb to go to sleep. I couldn't quite stand straight. The weight of longing was too much. Where was the boy who would sit with me and have me make the voices of his stuffed animals for hours while he laughed? Where was the boy who took walks with me, looking for dinosaur eggs (little rocks) and searching for hidden, invisible dinosaurs in the trees? Where was the boy who cuddled up to me in bed to watch *Shark Tale* for the 1,675th time?

Well, he was in his room, talking to Emily.

I know this is as it should be, and I know that it's a good thing. He needs to forge these relationships, and I couldn't be happier that he has such a close one with someone as awesome as Emily. But

I'm still sad. Sad that the chubby cheeks are gone, that my hair doesn't have tiny hands entwined in it.

But I'm happy too. Happy that he still wants to share the things he loves with me, that he still hugs me, laughs with me, and thinks I'm pretty cool. Happy that he has friends and is turning into an amazing young man.

I've been replaced. It's as it should be.

Please pass the chocolate.

"Wouldn't it be funny if Victoria's Secret was that she was really Victor?"

–Deep thoughts, by Me

Chapter 31

I Forgot

Not long ago, I bought a deck of UNO cards, thinking it would be fun to play with my boys. As a teen, I loved playing cards with my mom; they're some of my happiest memories.

I told Gavin I had them. He semi-nodded and went off to play. The cards sat on the counter for a week, and when the boys left on Friday to spend the week with their dad, the cards moved to the drawer.

In truth, I forgot about them.

A few nights later, we had the house to ourselves after spending the afternoon swimming. I'd taken Aidan and a friend of Gavin's to the store to get Aidan this epic shark water floaty thing he'd seen. He spent the first 20 minutes of pool time blowing it up, only to find it was better suited for a three-year-old. He sat it next to me, silently proclaiming "boredom." I told him he had to sit and wait until his brother and his friend had time to enjoy the pool, and so he did. He stared off into space, watched the people, kindly went and opened the tricky bathroom door so his brother could use the restroom. We sat in silence mostly, watching, lost in thought.

Once we got home, it didn't take long for the boys to start fighting and for me to start losing my temper. Their fighting saps my energy immediately and I lost it, yelling at them to stop. Dinner was a mishmash of thrown together items: grilled cheese and fruit for Aidan, quesadilla for me, and cereal and yogurt for Gavin. Oh, and cereal for the teen too, because he is getting to where he eats ALL-THEFOOD.

The day was another where I found myself thinking, "Can we just make it to Monday when school is in and routines are back and I don't feel the need to plan and entertain them?" Because yes, I am that mom who feels uneasy with down-time. I'm working on it, folks. No shame here.

After dinner, Aidan was outside, Gavin was sitting at the table having a treat, and I was tired. I wanted nothing more than to take a bath and read my book. Standing at the counter, I remembered the cards. I asked Gavin if he'd like to play, and he said okay. I opened the deck and was reading the instructions (since I'd totally forgotten how to play) when Aidan came in.

"What are you doing?" he asked.

"Playing UNO, but I don't remember the rules, and there are new cards in here I don't understand. Do you know how to play?"

He nodded and said, "Deal me in."

He showed us how to play. We laughed, we moaned, we high-fived each other. I won and did a little song and dance that made them smile. Aidan only has enough attention span for two games, so he bowed out but still stayed close, watching TV and chatting. Gavin and I proceeded to play THE LONGEST UNO GAME EVER and his joy was palpable. He sang a little ditty about how he was going to win (he did) and laughed, which made me laugh.

When he won, I said it was time for bed—and he didn't fight me on it. Instead, he asked if we could play tomorrow, then begged me to shuffle and deal out the cards so it would be all ready when he got up. I did. As he got ready for bed, he talked about the game and asked if we could play *as soon as* he got up. I agreed and lay down next to him. He smiled, covered me up, and rubbed my arm. His happiness filled me.

I spend a lot of nights reflecting on the days when I failed, on all the things I should have done or said. But I also replay that night I spent the evening smiling, laughing, and connecting with the boys. Over a card game. Not some elaborate outing or adventure. Nothing that involved buying them something, taking them somewhere, or filling the hours for them. We simply sat at home around our table and played cards.

I sometimes forget that it takes so little. I forget that joy doesn't always come from planning outings, or from buying them a new toy, like a shark meant for a three-year-old. It comes from spending time with them—seeing them, connecting, and being silly. Simply, lovingly, and wholly putting aside my to-do list, letting the dishes sit, and just *being* there.

Last night there was joy.

And this morning, waiting on the table, is another round of joy to be had with my boy.

Your son made honor roll, won his baseball tournament, AND completed the summer reading challenge already?
Mine used a napkin last night instead of his shirt.
Samesies.

Chapter 32

Strange Men at My Window

I was waiting at my ex's apartment for Aidan to come out. I was passing time on my phone, laughing with Howard Stern, and wondering what I was going to make for dinner. When I looked up to see if he was coming, I became irritated when the only person heading toward my car was some man and no Aidan. I had started dialing his cell phone, ready to launch into a tirade about how he needs to move faster so I don't have to wait so long, when I almost peed my pants. The man I'd seen walking was now knocking at my window.

I looked up and it hit me—this man was *Aidan!*

I unlocked the door for him and sat there speechless as he got in and asked me why I looked so spooked. But the voice asking me was a man's voice, deep, throaty, and full of . . . manliness. I mumbled something about being lost in thought, then spent the car drive home listening to him rave about the newest video game he was playing, silently thinking, "My baby is gone."

I truly don't like clichés, but this really did happen overnight. I woke up, went to get my little boy, and a man appeared at my window.

I'm no longer in control.

I no longer plan our weekend activities or take him with me everywhere. I no longer tuck him into bed with a story and cuddles as he falls asleep. I don't wash his hair, make bubble hats for him, or fill the bath with plastic dinosaur toys. And I don't know when each of those things stopped. They've been only memories for so long now that they're merely movie clips of the past in my head. What's heartbreaking is that so many of these memories will be mine alone; he already says he doesn't remember all the sweetness of his childhood that I do.

Good God, the tears are heavy right now. His childhood is gone and I can't get it back (and asking my 14-year-old to play with my hair and suck his thumb to go to sleep solely for memory's sake is probably out).

There are no little boy hands. The braces he's been wearing for over a year have corrected his serious overbite, so his jaw is strong and aligned and his eyes are more knowing. He's covered in all things teenager—meaning acne, oily hair, stinky teen smell, and CHANGE! Frankly, I'm not sure how to handle it.

But despite how horrid teen years can be, so far with Aidan, they've been really nice. We talk about everything from girls and video games to my childhood memories and how to manage money. He still asks me for my opinion, and recently, as he was navigating the treacherous path of having his first girlfriend, he asked me a lot about why girls do certain things, what they think, and how the whole relationship thing is supposed to work. I didn't have all the answers, but that's not the point. The point is that he still talks to me. He still values my opinion, still hugs me, still tells me I look nice when I put a dress on. But it doesn't change the fact that my little boy is gone.

It also doesn't mean that he doesn't have secrets. He does. There will never be a time in his life again where I know him like I used to—his sleeping, eating, playing, crying, and even pooping schedule (that one I'm okay with letting go). I'll never again hear all of his nightmares and sweet dreams, and I won't always know the perfect gift for his birthday or Christmas. I won't know how to fix his hurts, because a Band-Aid, a kiss, and marshmallows can't solve grown-up hurts.

It makes me hold a little tighter to Gavin. I'm trying to be more present, to cherish each night-time cuddle and the way he still comes to me when he's hurt. I'm trying, but I'm also failing. There are nights when I'm tired, wanting nothing more than to fall into bed and sleep away the day's frustrations, wishing Gavin would just go to sleep without me there next to him. Then I wake in the morning and want nothing more than for him to come into my bed and cuddle. But he's already up, active and tackling the day. Yes, he's still a little boy, but I see the changes coming this time. His face is becoming less childlike, his hands stronger. His eyes know a little more each day.

I wish motherhood weren't such a tangle of how you want things to be, woven in with reality and pulled tight with daily stresses, worries, regrets, and change. The saving grace is that with this knot of reality is the knowledge that the knot can be undone, leaving you with fine fibers of joy, learning, and more love than you ever thought possible.

And strange men. You're left with strange men you now need to get to know.

Told my son he needed to clean his room. He informed me the stuff on his floor is "art" and probably worth millions to someone.
Hope that someone likes their "art" in a trash bag.

Chapter 33

Keep It Clean, Ladies

Lately, I've noticed when visiting friends that the art of keeping a clean house seems to have gone out of fashion. I'm embarrassed for my friends when I visit, seeing their dirty dishes filling the sink with sadness, their laundry pile a warm bed for their dog or cat, and the kids' stuff everywhere. I usually try to casually comment, how it looks like they must be swamped with work/life/school as I glance around. I don't want to be rude, but I do raise my brows a bit.

What's happened with women today? Where is their pride, their desire to show their love through actions and not just words?

When I was young, my mom kept the house immaculate. She spent every Saturday morning cleaning. From top to bottom that house sparkled, and Lord help the human who came in without removing their shoes or who set stuff on the couch.

She also ironed everything, stopping short of underwear. Even her jeans were perfectly pressed. She was the epitome of the woman who could do it all: cook, clean, work outside the home, and look amazing while doing it. Her hair and makeup were perfectly done daily, even Sundays. She was the woman I aspired to be.

My mother worked hard until five p.m., when she allowed herself a small respite to sit at the kitchen table with her favorite box of cookies (she only allowed herself one small box a night). She would ask me to give her space while she relaxed, and I did. In my eyes, she managed to do it all, happily. (Okay, I did find her crying a few times, but I was sure she'd just finished a sad book or something.)

She made me see that a clean house reflects a pride of ownership, and a pride in who you are as a person. She taught me well, and now I keep a clean house. To be honest, I love it. I love the feeling of watching the dirty dishes sparkle (I only wash by hand), and when I sweep, it's a calming workout ritual for me. Picking up the kids' toys/ socks/clothes/dirtydishes/shoes/papers/gum-wrappers/games/underwear/socks/socks/socks, I stop to allow the blessed feelings wash over me, because I get to do all of this for my kids, whom I love more than anything.

Keeping a clean house for my husband and cooking him dinner is the highlight of my day. Seeing the joy on his face while he eats my labor of love has no comparison. When my boys cry that they're going to die from the grossness of my labor of love, I happily get up and cook a second kid-friendly dinner for them. *That's* what love is about. *That* is being a woman.

THAT is a load of CRAP.

I despise cleaning, and hell will freeze over before I cook a second meal.

Okay, it wasn't *so* bad before I had kids, when at least I could clean and know it would remain somewhat tidy for a few days. But once the kids came, it became fruitless.

When they were little, if I cleaned the kitchen, it was only a matter of time before they came in wanting to take out the pots and pans to bang on them. Now that they're older, they come in to fix a snack (because they never stop eating these days), which means emptying the fridge and cupboard of ALLTHETHINGS and then forgetting where everything goes.

I stopped trying to keep a clean kitchen.

Bathrooms used to be somewhat safe when the boys were younger, since they were only in there to bathe. Once they were potty trained, however, the bathroom became the URINE DEPOSITORY FROM HELL. I never thought I would stand in my bathroom and yell, "How in the hell did pee get on the ceiling?" Apparently, it is possible. And on the walls, door, and even the windows.

Bathrooms were added to my "Do Not Bother" list.

I decided once they got a bit older that they were capable of cleaning their own rooms. Thursday evening is room-cleaning time, and they're not allowed any games or TV until it's done. I thought things were going pretty well until I went into my teen's room recently to put a few things in his closet, and I couldn't get the closet door open. When I questioned him he said, "Yeah, it doesn't open anymore. I put too much stuff in there and it all fell over and blocked the door." Let me tell you how enjoyable it was getting that door open. And once it was open, there was a stench like rotting, horrible, something-in-there-must-be-dead stink. Turns out the miniature pumpkins we drew faces on last Halloween hadn't been thrown away after all. They'd just been thrown in the closet.

Kids room—hell, no.

I then started doing the "Hubby Home Hustle," where I would wait until 20 minutes before my husband was due to be home, then rush around and wipe counters (not well), throw things in closets (kids can teach adults some things), and spray Febreeze all over everything, especially around the front door. Then, because I am all about equality in marriage, I'd tell my hubby that I was so tired from work and cleaning that I needed him to make dinner and clean up. Win! But in truth, the dirt was still there, the pee was still on the ceiling, and Febreeze only masks the smells for so long.

Finally, sitting in my closet one night, enjoying the box of See's I'd bought that day, it dawned on me: I'm *done* trying to clean! I figure I work, take care of the kids, grocery shop, make lunches, do laundry . . . I'm pretty much superwoman in all aspects except cleaning. I decided right then, I'm not cleaning. I'll keep things tidy, but scrubbing and mopping are history.

It's been almost 14 years since I gave up on cleaning. It was so monumental that I remember the day: September 13, 2003. That was the day an angel of mercy walked into my life—with white sneakers, a broom, and a smile—and cleaned my house for me. Let me repeat—*she cleaned my house for me.* I hired a savior, a sanity saver, a clean-smelling, wondrous woman who saved my life. We've since become close, so I made a lifelong friend in the process. I say a gratitude prayer for her daily.

I do *not* apologize for not cleaning my house. I do not apologize for letting someone else clean my toilets. I do not apologize for letting go of the idea that I have to spend my free time scrubbing and washing.

I *do* sometimes apologize for the insane amounts of pee on *everything* in the bathrooms, and the odd smells in the boys' rooms. But that's it.

I'd like to say I have my act together.
Then I step in the dog poo I'm trying to pick up and swallow a bug on my walk.

Chapter 34

Sneaky Ways to Relax

Established: My world consists of everything "boy." My days are filled with fighting, flatulence, food preparation, and forgetting where I put my glasses. I usually find them on my head but once, they were in the refrigerator. Being a blogger, I am constantly online finding the day's hot topics, new research showing why wine and chocolate lead to longer lives (that would be the longer lives of the men in my life, because those two things keep me sane), and studies that tell me how I'm doing everything wrong.

By the end of the day, I'm beat. My hair is a mess, I've lost my cool more than once, and I have dinner remnants on my finding pants*. I decided all those articles about how moms need to find time for themselves so they can be the best for their children have some merit. And so, I've spent serious time figuring out ways to carve out me time and relax. I'm nothing if not diligent and determined, so I was going to find ways to relax if it killed me!

Here are my top three (sneaky) ways to relax:

1. Laundry Watch: I've done a disservice to my future daughters-in-law, but in my defense, this *needed* to be done. I plan to reveal the truth when my boys are 15 and 10, but not before then. I've told them that our washer and dryer are top-of-the-line energy savers that require someone physically there during the washing and drying process to "push the energy-saving buttons." They both think this is the worst possible torture—having to sit in the laundry room—so they leave me alone. This avoids the possibility of them asking to cover my watch. I have a stash of cookies, a nice bottle of red and my fancy wine glass, magazines, and a folding chair. I keep the door closed and relish my hidey hole. Then I make them fold the laundry because I'm so tired from keeping watch.

2. SPIDERS!: My boys are typical boys. Farting, burping, fighting, eating, and they stink no matter how often they shower. But when it comes to spiders, my boys will scream and run, flail their arms, and if it's big enough, cry. We have a deck out back with a great view. I like to sit out there in the sun, and I don't want to hear all about Halo and Pokémon the whole time. Solution: spiders! I came running in screaming one day because there really was a spider (where do you think my boys learned to be screaming girls?). I told them there was the biggest spider ever out there on the deck. My husband killed it (I love him so much) and since then, my boys will not set foot on our deck. I spend a lot of time out there because, I told them, I have outgrown my fear of spiders. God forbid I ever see one out there again, but so far, so good.

3. Foot Rubs: I love nothing more than a good foot rub. Since I haven't won the lottery and can't hire a full-time foot rubber, I devised a sneaky way to get my boys to do it. They love their video games, so I instituted "Hands-On Gaming." They earn gaming time for hands-on time—on my feet! I'm not mean, so I make it worthwhile. For every five minutes of foot rubbing, they get 15 minutes of gaming time. The first time my teen rubbed my feet, it was over before I'd even blinked. But he's gotten better over time and has more stamina, and I find it's a great way to bond. Plus, creating good foot rubbers might make up for the laundry issue with my future daughters-in-law.

I'm sure I could just yell at my boys to go away. Or be the good mother who sits them down and explains that Mommy time is vital, and could they please respect my time and occupy themselves? (Okay, that one made me choke on my coffee a little.) But I choose this way. I'm sneaky and sure I'm doing it all wrong but hey, I'm relaxed in my wrongness and therefore delivering the best possible me to my children.

Someday, when they have kids and find themselves pushing the laundry buttons or hanging out with spiders, they will thank me. (I'll take my thanks in the form of a foot rub, please.)

*Finding pants look very much like yoga pants, but c'mon, yoga? Ha! I spend all my time in them finding things: my glasses, my son's thingy, the dog's toy, my coffee cup. *Finding pants.*

Parenting basically means that when I look hungover in the morning, it has nothing to do with booze or a good time and most likely involved poop.

Chapter 35

I'm Done . . . For Now

As of this writing, my now 14-year-old has fallen in love (not ready, not ready, not ready), and my younger son just told me he's a vegetarian. But NOT a vegetablenarian.

Also, he hates vegetables.

My eldest has assured me he doesn't need to go to college because he plans to work at Microsoft as a game tester. Noodle on that one for a bit, will ya.

I'm in school to become a life and writing coach, where hopefully I will be able to work with other moms and give them a safe haven to escape the crazy that comes with motherhood. I hope to listen, hold their secret stories, and show them ways to change those stories so they are no longer heavy burdens.

Since I don't have a crystal ball, I obviously have no idea what the future holds. I know change will be inevitable, as will continued flatulence, smells, and for the foreseeable future, me yelling, "Brush your teeth!!!" twice a day. My hope is that oral hygiene will become more important since Aidan is thinking about girls. Nonstop.

I know I will have days where I hide. I will have days where I feel like superwoman (kind of like right now, since writing this book has been my dream since forever and I can't believe I'm writing the final chapter!). I will have days when I cry, because where my boys once stood, I now see young men. I will encounter frustration, fear, joy, and most of all love.

Always the love.

About the Author

Heather is an imperfect human trying to raise perfect humans. She's mom to 2 boys of her own and a step-son. She lives in the gross world of boys who argue about using soap in the shower and ensure the dog always has fun stuff to lick in the bathroom.

Heather writes to connect women who feel alone, who are missing a village of support. She writes for the mother of a special needs child who's not sure how she is going to manage one more meltdown, one more parent-teacher conference, or one more day. She writes for the women who pee their pants when they sneeze, cry during commercials for diapers, and who still want to sometimes hear, "You're pretty."

Follow the funny on FB at https://www.facebook.com/tipsytiaras

Read the latest and greatest on her blog at http://www.tipsytiaras.com

See her embarrassing photos on Instagram at http://www.instagram.com/tipsytiaras